CRUCIAL AMERICAN
ELECTIONS

Memoirs of the

AMERICAN PHILOSOPHICAL SOCIETY

Held at Philadelphia

For Promoting Useful Knowledge

Volume 99

CRUCIAL
AMERICAN
ELECTIONS

Symposium presented at the Autumn General Meeting
of the American Philosophical Society

November 10, 1972

AMERICAN PHILOSOPHICAL SOCIETY
INDEPENDENCE SQUARE • PHILADELPHIA

1973

The publication of this book was aided by
the John Louis Haney Publication Fund
of the American Philosophical Society.

Foreword

THIS BOOK consists of papers read at a symposium on crucial American elections before the American Philosophical Society on November 10, 1972. The authors are all distinguished specialists in their fields. Merrill D. Peterson, Thomas Jefferson Professor of History at the University of Virginia, is one of the leading Jefferson scholars in the United States. Joel H. Silbey, who has been applying the new methods of research in quantified data to the American political system in the antebellum period with significant results, is Professor of History at Cornell University. Don E. Fehrenbacher, Professor of History at Stanford University, is a leading Lincoln scholar, concentrating upon the war President's rise to greatness and his methods of leadership. Gilbert C. Fite, long-time Research Professor of History at the University of Oklahoma and now President of Eastern Illinois University, has devoted a life time of scholarship to the history of American agriculture and agrarian politics. Donald R. McCoy, Professor of History at the University of Kansas, has enriched the literature of recent American history with biographies of Calvin Coolidge and Alfred M. Landon.

Presidential politics—the struggle for the presidency and the privilege of determining national policies—has been the biggest business in the United States since the formation of the national government under the Constitution. It has also been the most decisive, because almost all important questions in our democratic society are finally solved in the political arena, with the President playing a large role in their resolution. However, some presidential elections have surely been more crucial than others. For example, the election of 1796 merely assured the continuation of Federalist policies, while the election of 1800, as Professor Peterson reminds us, resulted in the first peaceful transfer of power from one party to another and marked the beginning of an entirely new type of national politics. The election of 1860, as Professor Fehrenbacher has said, was not only crucial but catastrophic in its outcome—southern secession and a long and bloody civil war. Professor Fite has made clear that the election of 1896 marked the final victory of the city over the country and the beginning of urban-oriented presidential politics. It also saw the triumph of the advocates of law and order over the combined forces of discontent. The election of 1932, as Professor McCoy has written, was of course important, but it was not so crucial as the election of 1936. In the former, the voters merely registered their discontent with the Hoover administration and their hopes for better days ahead. In the election of 1936, on the other hand, they gave emphatic approval to the New Deal and a sweeping mandate for the continuation of Roosevelt's policies, and they established the Democrats as the majority party for decades to come.

Some elections have been more crucial than historians have been wont to observe. Professor Silbey demonstrates this observation in his essay on the much-neglected election of 1836. Historians have conventionally been attracted to the more exciting presidential battle of 1832, when the common people gave an overwhelming victory to Andrew Jackson in his battle against the Bank of the United States. Yet the election of 1836 resulted in changes more important than four years before—the institutionalization and professionalization of American politics and the emergence of a definite two-party system, which would hereafter characterize the political structure and history of the United States.

The papers that follow are full of analysis, interpretation, and insight.   Taken together, they provide a remarkable overview of American national politics from the early days of the republic to the 1930's.   The American Philosophical Society is deeply indebted to their authors for making this volume possible.

ARTHUR S. LINK
Edwards Professor of American History
Princeton University

February 28, 1973

Contents

The Election of 1800

THE INAUGURATION of Thomas Jefferson as president of
the United States on March 4, 1801, completed the
first democratic transfer of power in the nation's history,
indeed in the history of modern politics. By the con-
stitutional process of a free election, the opposition party
led by Jefferson, the Republican, displaced the ruling
party, the Federalist, which had dominated the government from its inception twelve years before. Such an
event, however ordinary it may appear to us, was anything
but ordinary in its time and in its consequences. The
Federalist leaders conceived of themselves as a ruling class,
as the guardians of the government they had established,
and they denied any title of legitimacy to their opponents.
The script had not yet been written for a democratic
succession. The Federalist ideal has been well described
as "a speaking aristocracy in the face of a silent democracy." [1] When the Jeffersonians went outside the government and built a political party in the broad electorate,
thus giving voice to the "silent democracy," they set up a
different ideal, one that saw in the agitation and organization of public opinion the vital principle of American
government. Because the Jeffersonians were successful,
the Constitution became an instrument of democracy,
change became possible without violence or destruction,
and the process began by which the government could go
forward with the ongoing consent of the governed. The
election of 1800 was therefore *critical* in the most basic
sense: it secured all the elections to come.

[1] David Hackett Fisher, *The Revolution of American Conservatism* (New
York, 1965), p. 4.

1

How this came about is, of course, a long story. The Constitution was intended to work without parties. In every free government, the framers said, various *factions* or *interests* compete for political power, but government may be constituted in such a way as to "break the violence of faction" and prevent any single faction, or party, from becoming dominant. The Constitution would have this tendency for a number of reasons, above all because its jurisdiction extended to such an immense territory with so many jarring interests that the organization of a majority party would be virtually impossible. Political parties in competition for the suffrages of the people were anathema to the framers. Parties fed on the turbulence of the populace and served the ambitions of demagogues; they caused implacable rivalries in legislative councils, usurping the place of reason and moderation; they introduced whole networks of partisan allegiance at cross purposes with the national welfare. Parties were thought to be especially dangerous in the young American republic because of the weakness of established authorities to check or awe the populace; because they must tend to divide the people along sectional lines, further jeopardizing the already precarious union; and because foreign nations, drawing the new transatlantic republic into the power-balance of the Old World, would seek to subvert these parties to their own use.

Yet political parties soon formed on great issues of domestic and foreign policy in President Washington's administration. These issues need not detain us. The important point is that a political opposition arose and that the legitimacy of this opposition became the issue fundamental to everything else. What was at stake from the perspective of 1800 was the process by which a political minority is allowed to oppose the administration in power, convert itself into a new majority, and win control of the government. By the way the antagonists positioned themselves on this issue, they revealed incompatible conceptions of political parties and disclosed a wide gulf between two systems of politics, one closed and elitist, the other open and democratic.

The Federalists have been called, in Max Weber's phrase, "a party of notables." [2] Men of established property and position for the most part, they had a vested interest in social order and were accustomed to clubbing together politically. They had a powerful nucleus, the mercantile community of the coastal cities, to which the measures of the new government made a strong appeal. The Federalists might manipulate public opinion, but they distrusted it, spoke condescendingly of "the people," and sought to counteract the government's vulnerability to opinion. The Republican party, while not lacking in "notables," was without a nucleus. It found its strength in the latent power of numbers. The socially given elitism and cohesiveness of the Federalists would be overcome by a broadbased and heterogeneous party in the electorate. The Republicans extended the bounds of public participation in the political process and opened channels to popular agitation. Not "influence" at court but opinion in the country became, in their view, the vital force of republican government.

To some extent, certainly, the clash between these two systems was epitomized in the conflict between Jefferson and Hamilton. One despised, the other idolized, rulership. One located the strength of the republic in the diffuse energies of a free society, the other in the consolidation of the government's power. One cherished the people as "the best bloodhounds of tyrants," the other feared the people lest their natural "turbulence" shake the founda-

[2] William Nisbet Chambers, *Political Parties in a New Nation* (New York, 1963), pp. 44, 106.

tions of authority. Hamilton thought the Constitution "a shilly shally thing" too feeble to survive except by every possible reinforcement, which he proceeded to supply. Jefferson considered the Constitution an inviolable trust given by the people, a superintending rule of political action rather than a point of departure for heroic statesmanship. He believed that private interest corrupted public good, while Hamilton, the ghost of Mandeville looking over his shoulder, enlisted private vices for public benefits. For the Hamiltonians, government was to save the people from their own worst enemy, themselves; for the Jeffersonians, government *was* the enemy except as it embodied the will of the people.

The question of the legitimacy of opposition, together with the government's responsibility to public opinion, was never far from the surface. As early as December, 1790, the Virginia General Assembly protested the Federalist program for funding the debt, calling it unconstitutional, designed to perpetuate "a large monied interest," and "fatal to the existence of American liberty." [3] Hamilton, the author of the program, greeted the Virginia resolutions with gestures of defiance. "This is the first symptom of a spirit which must either be killed or will kill the Constitution of the United States," he said.[4] As Hamilton rapidly brought forward the other measures of his system, it became apparent that one of the grounds of complaint concerned, not the right or wrong of the measures by themselves, but their magisterial presumption on the opinion of the country. Hamilton and his cadre in Congress supposed they were strengthening the new government when, in fact, they were undermining its only sure foundation in the consent of the governed.

[3] See Henry S. Commager, ed., *Documents of American History* (New York 1946) 1: pp. 155–156.
[4] Hamilton to John Jay, November 13, 1970, in Harold Syrett, ed., *The Papers of Alexander Hamilton* (New York, 1961–) 7: p. 149.

But how were issues to be articulated publicly and popular consent to be mobilized? The country was so vast, the arts of communication were so primitive, it was hard to see how a responsive public opinion could be formed, yet the future of republican government depended on it. Facing this problem in 1791, Jefferson and Madison established a newspaper, *The National Gazette,* which was intended to counteract the court newspaper in the capital and also to circulate through the country as a "Whig vehicle of intelligence." It was a bold move, resting squarely on the proposition earlier enunciated by Jefferson. "The people are the only censors of their governors," he said, "and even their errors will tend to keep these to the true principles of their institution." The way to put the people in the right is to bring them into the political process:

> to give them full information of their affairs through the channel of the public papers, and to contrive that those papers should penetrate the whole mass of the people. The basis of our governments being the opinion of the people, the very object should be to keep that right; and were it left to me to decide whether we should have a government without newspapers, or newspapers without a government, I should not hesitate a moment to prefer the latter.[5]

But the Federalist leaders, Hamilton at the head, felt threatened by *The National Gazette* and launched a campaign to discredit it as a tool of faction tending to subvert the government.

The press was not the only vehicle employed by the Republicans to move the public mind. In 1793, when the old monarchical enemy, Great Britain, was at war with the new French republic, they seized upon the spontaneous outburst of so-called "democratic societies" to advance their cause. These societies—thirty-eight of them across the country—were similar to the corresponding societies

[5] Jefferson to Edward Carrington, January 16, 1787, in Julian P. Boyd, ed., *The Papers of Thomas Jefferson* (Princeton, 1950–   ) 11: p. 49.

before the American Revolution, but their impetus was another revolution, the French, and they sought to channel popular enthusiasm for that revolution abroad into the Republican cause at home. The Federalists linked the societies to the notorious Jacobin Clubs of Paris, branded them seditious, and aimed at their destruction. And the Federalists succeeded, first by implicating them in the Whiskey Rebellion of 1794 and then—the crushing blow—by President Washington's public condemnation of the societies as illicit political engines. Jefferson, now in retirement at Monticello, was shocked: "It is wonderful indeed, that the President should have permitted himself to be the organ of such an attack on the freedom of discussion, the freedom of writing, printing and publishing." [6] Two years later, in his Farewell Address, Washington again betrayed intolerance of political opposition from outside the official channels of government. Organized parties came between the people and their representatives, distracted the public councils, agitated the community with ill-founded jealousies and alarms, and so on. Their effects were "baneful," Washington declared, and their spirit should never be encouraged in an elective government. But the Republicans, of course, were coming to see democratic party organization as the appropriate mechanism for wresting the government from the high-handed and quasi-monarchical Federalists.

As long as Washington was president, so great was the confidence he inspired that the opposition was checked. But no halo surrounded John Adams; his theoretical opinions were suspiciously "monarchical"; and his accession coincided with a burgeoning crisis with France which deepened the party conflict. When agents of the French republic attempted to swindle the Americans sent to nego-

[6] Jefferson to James Madison, December 28, 1794, in Paul L. Ford, ed., *The Writings of Thomas Jefferson* (New York, 1892–1899) 6: pp. 516–517.

tiate in Paris (the XYZ Affair), the Federalists chose to convert the foreign crisis into a domestic crisis. Under cover of a whipped-up war hysteria, they attacked the patriotism of the Republicans, portrayed them as Jacobin disorganizers in the country's bowels, and moved to silence their presses. Adams, relishing his new-found popularity, inflamed the spirit of intolerance by bombastic answers to the numerous addresses of loyalty pouring into Philadelphia. Not only the French, and sundry aliens, especially the Irish, but his own fellow citizens were the enemy. Adams assailed "the delusions and misrepresentations of party," "the calumnies and contempt against Constituted Authorities," "the profligate spirit of falsehood and malignity" against the government, and declared that "the degraded and deluded characters may tremble, lest they should be condemned to the severest punishment an American suffers—that of being conveyed in safety within the lines of an invading enemy."[7] It was enough to plunge Madison into melancholy reflection on the old truth, which perhaps not even the most favored nation of God's footstool would escape, "that the loss of liberty at home is to be charged to provisions against dangers real or pretended abroad."[8]

The crucial measure of the Federalist program was the Sedition Act of July, 1798. Its advocates believed that government, and governors, can be criminally assaulted by opinion and that government has an inherent right to protect itself, indeed to protect the people themselves whose government it is, by punishing opinion deemed false, scandalous, or malicious. This is what the Sedition Act proposed to do. The Republican minority in Congress,

[7] Jefferson to James Madison, May 3, 1798, in Ford, ed., *Writings* 7: p. 247; Manning J. Dauer, *The Adams Federalists* (Baltimore, 1953), p. 161; Charles F. Adams, ed., *The Works of John Adams* (Boston, 1850–1856) 9: p. 196.

[8] Madison to Thomas Jefferson, May 13, 1798, in *Letters and Other Writings of James Madison.* Congress Edition (Washington, 1894) 2: p. 140.

considerably reduced now because of the war hysteria, denied that the government was threatened by the free circulation of opinion; even if it was, the First Amendment protected freedom of speech and press. Moreover, some Republicans argued, freedom to criticize the government was essential to hold it responsible to the people, to command their confidence, and to secure the avenues of peaceful change. No Republican doubted that the act looked to the suppression of the feeble party press. The sequel confirmed their fears. Twenty-five persons were arrested under the Sedition Act, fourteen indicted, and ten tried and convicted, principally Republican printers and publicists. Scarcely an opposition newspaper north of the Potomac escaped this "reign of terror." The damage from intimidation was incalculable. If the law went unresisted, new repressive measures, probably involving the use of the army that had been raised to combat an illusory foreign foe, must follow. Yet it was difficult to know how to resist. The executive, both houses of Congress, and the entire judicial establishment were in Federalist hands. There was no *official* channel through which redress could be had. In this situation, Jefferson and Madison turned to the state legislatures. The Virginia and Kentucky Resolutions of 1798 interposed the authority of these states, declared both Alien and Sedition Acts unconstitutional, and appealed to the other legislatures to seek their repeal. Whatever the later significance of these famous resolutions for the issue of state rights and union—the issue on which the Civil War would be fought—they originated in a desperate struggle for political survival and addressed the fundamental issue of freedom and self-government descending from the American Revolution.

The crisis with France passed in 1799. Congress, nevertheless, reaffirmed the Sedition Act, thereby keeping the gun at Republican heads during the ensuing presidential election.   In January, 1800, Senator James Ross of Pennsylvania introduced legislation setting forth procedures to be followed by Congress when it came to scrutinize the electoral vote cast in the states.   A joint committee elected by the two houses would meet in secret session, throw out votes deemed irregular or bad, and submit its report, which would be final, to Congress.   Of course, Federalists would control the committee.   Fortunately, this blatant party measure failed in the House after passing the Senate. When it was still before the Senate, where debates were secret, the Republican editor in Philadelphia, William Duane, got hold of the bill and published it.   Duane had already been twice arraigned under the Sedition Act only to squirm free each time.   Now the Federalist senators summoned him before the bar of the House to answer for the publication.   (He would finally slip out of this noose too.)   Political shenanigans looking to the election were not confined to Congress.   In New York, as in several other states, the legislature chose the presidential electors. After the Republicans won the state election in April, 1800, Hamilton urged the governor, John Jay, to convene the lame-duck Federalist legislature in order to change the electoral law and thus contrive to nullify the Republican verdict.   Otherwise, he warned, the country faced "a revolution after the manner of Bonaparte." [9]   But there was honor among Federalists, and Jay quietly buried the proposal.

The election of 1800 was the first in which two organized parties openly contested the presidency of the United States.   It was bitterly fought on both sides.   Everyone seemed to understand that the outcome would fix the political destiny of the country for decades to come. Around Jefferson the Republicans achieved unprecedented unity of action and feeling.   "Image" was no less important

[9] Hamilton to John Jay, May 7, 1800, in Henry Cabot Lodge, ed., *The Works of Alexander Hamilton* (New York, 1904) **10**: p. 372.

then than now; and Jefferson was imaged as the democratic "man of the people," while John Adams was draped in the hideous garments of kings and nobles. Through the apparatus of party organization the Republicans mobilized opinion at the country crossroads and in the city wards. Federalists were astounded. "Every threshing floor," one of them wrote, "every husking, every party work on a house-frame or raising a building, the very funerals are infected with bawlers and whisperers against government." [10] Distrusting democracy, the Federalist "notables" were ill equipped to conduct a campaign in the electorate. Their war system, with its engines of terrorizing public opinion, was collapsing around them in 1800; and scheming Hamiltonian Federalists turned in sullen anger upon the president who had courageously made peace with France. Divided, dismayed, desperate, the Federalists could nonetheless cordially unite in a campaign of vilification against Jefferson. And vilify him they did, as a hardhearted infidel, as a Jacobin incendiary, an unscrupulous demagogue, a visionary, an abolitionist, and the enemy of Washington, the Union, and the Constitution. Under him, surely, the churches would be destroyed and the nation laid waste by revolutionary fanaticism. "Murder, robbery, rape, adultery, and incest will openly be taught and practiced," wrote one pamphleteer, "the air will be rent with the cries of distress, the soil will be soaked with blood, and the nation black with crimes." [11] (This, it should be remembered, came from men who considered it a crime to speak ill of Federalist magistrates.) The Federalists swept New England, took two of the small middle states (New Jersey and Delaware), and picked up scattered votes in three other states, but the Republicans won everything else, south, west,

[10] In Seth Ames, ed., *The Works of Fisher Ames* (Boston, 1854) 2: p. 115.
[11] Quoted in Charles O. Lerche, "Jefferson and the Election of 1800: A Case Study of the Political Smear," *William and Mary Quart.*, 3rd. ser., 5 (1948): p. 480.

and north. The electoral vote, 73 to 65, failed to reflect the wide margin of the Republican victory at the polls.

Unfortunately, the victory was jeopardized by a treacherous abyss in the electoral system. The Twelfth Amendment providing separate ballots for president and vice-president had yet to be enacted. Jefferson and his running-mate, Aaron Burr, received an equal number of electoral votes, and under the Constitution the choice between them must be made by the House of Representatives. There the lame-duck Federalist majority, defiant to the end, plotted to annul the popular verdict either by creating an interregnum or by dealing Burr into the presidency. Burr, if he did not condone the latter scheme, acquiesced in it. As the crisis mounted, Republican zealots in neighboring states threatened to march on Washington to put down any man bold enough to offer himself as a usurper. Finally, on the thirty-sixth ballot in the House, the stalemate was broken and Jefferson was elected. "Thus has ended," Albert Gallatin remarked, "the most wicked . . . attempt ever tried by the Federalists"—their last attempt to control the government in the face of public opinion.[12]

Jefferson's First Inaugural Address may be read both as an epilogue to this long political ordeal and as a prologue to things to come. It was a lofty summation of the Republican creed: the principles of this creed Jefferson traced back to the American Revolution and pledged himself to make them once again the touchstone of American government. It was a bold bid for the restoration of harmony and affection: "We have called by different names brethren of the same principle. We are all republicans: we are all federalists." Jefferson believed that the mass of Americans, excepting only the madcap Federalists, were fundamentally united in their political sentiments, and so there was no excuse for the hatreds and fanaticism—the insignia of

[12] Gallatin to Hannah Gallatin, February 17, 1801, in Henry Adams, ed., *The Writings of Albert Gallatin* (Philadelphia, 1879) 1: p. 262.

European politics—that had rocked the republic in recent years. Finally, the First Inaugural was a commitment to ongoing political change through the democratic process of open debate, popular participation, and free elections. This was the authentic "revolution of 1800." Jefferson named "absolute acquiescence in the decisions of the majority, the vital principle of republics, from which there is no appeal but to force." This principle, to be effective, demanded freedom of opinion. "If there be any among us," he said, alluding to the delusions of '98, "who would wish to dissolve this Union or to change its republican form, let them stand undisturbed as monuments of the safety with which error may be tolerated where reason is left free to combat it." Federalist leaders had reckoned the strength of government on Old World standards: army and navy, aristocratic establishments, the patronage of "the rich, the well born, and the able," great treasury, ministerial mastery, central command, the panoply of office and the splendor of state. But Jefferson called the American government, for all its feebleness by these standards, "the strongest government on earth" because it was the only one founded on the affections, the opinions, and the suffrages of the people.

Jefferson's faith would be severely tested during his presidency, yet he stuck to it. The churches were not destroyed; vice was not enthroned. Reins of power were slackened but peace and order prevailed. Rather than purge the Federalists from office, Jefferson sought to convert them to Republicanism. Even after partisan pressures forced him to revise this strategy, moderation marked his course and political amalgamation remained his goal. In certain quarters the Federalists held out, partly because they swallowed their pride and set out to emulate the Republican practices they despised, becoming, to that extent, a popular rather than an elitist party. But Jefferson won a landslide victory in 1804 when only Connecticut and

Delaware registered in the Federalist column. Nationally, the Federalists were never a viable *second* party and they slowly withered away. The election of 1800, far from beginning, put off for a quarter century permanent two-party competition in the American political system.

What was secured in 1800 was the political freedom that is the lifeblood of democratic politics. Before a steady stream of defamation and libel emanating from the Federalist press, Jefferson occasionally seemed to waiver, wondering whether some corrective was not in order to save the press from its abominable excesses; but he checked himself and adhered to what he came to call his "experiment" in unmolested freedom of discussion. In 1804 he wrote:

> No experiment can be more interesting than that we are now trying, and which we trust will end in establishing the fact, that man may be governed by reason and truth. Our first object should therefore be, to leave open to him all the avenues of truth. The most effectual hitherto found, is the freedom of the press. It is, therefore, the first shut up by those who fear investigation of their actions.

He went on to speak of the demonstrated ability of the people to sift truth from the mass of error and of the folly of attempting to dazzle them with pomp and splendor or deceive them with lies. "I hold it, therefore, certain," he concluded, "that to open the doors of truth and to fortify the habit of testing everything by reason, are the most effectual manacles we can rivet on the hand of our successors to prevent their manacling the people with their own consent." [13] The experiment proved itself. The principle was riveted on Jefferson's successors. And this was the critical, the enduring, importance of the election of 1800.

Merrill D. Peterson
Thomas Jefferson Professor of History,
University of Virginia

[13] Jefferson to John Tyler, June 28, 1804, in A. A. Lipscomb and A. E. Bergh, eds., *The Writings of Thomas Jefferson* (Washington, 1903) 11: p. 33.

The Election of 1836

THE ELECTION of 1836 remains dim or forgotten to most of us.[1] It lacked the drama of the revolution of 1800, or the pre-secession contest of 1860, the battle of the standards in 1896 or the first referendum on the New Deal forty years later. Indeed even observers at the time had serious doubts about it. To John Quincy Adams, "the remarkable character of this election, is that all the candidates are at most third rate men whose pretensions rest neither upon high attainment nor upon eminent services, but upon intrigue and political speculation." [2]

However, as shorn of drama or momentous aftermath as it was, the 1836 election was crucial in shaping and defining America's nineteenth-century political culture. It significantly advanced the organizational revolution underway in American politics and helped burn into the electorate's consciousness deep-seated commitments to each major party.[3] In all of these it had more significance than many better remembered elections.

Before Andrew Jackson's triumph in 1828, American politics had for some time been highly localized without

[1] A more detailed description of the election of 1836 is in Joel H. Silbey, "Election of 1836," in Arthur M. Schlesinger, Jr., *History of American Presidential Elections, 1789–1968* (New York, 1971) 1: pp. 577–642. There is no single book published about the election of 1836 but a doctoral dissertation has recently been completed on the topic. See Sister Mary R. Bartus, "The Presidential Election of 1836" (Ph.D., Fordham University, 1967).

[2] Allan Nevins (ed.), *The Diary of John Quincy Adams, 1794–1845* (New York, 1928), p. 471.

[3] Richard McCormick, "Political Development and the Second Party System," in William Nisbet Chambers and Walter Dean Burnham, *The American Party Systems* (New York, 1968), and McCormick's book, *The Second American Party System* (Chapel Hill, 1966), remain the outstanding introduction to party formation and electoral analysis in this period. In the following discussion, I have relied on McCormick's work extensively as a guide and for insights into many aspects of political development.

much national focus. National party organizations and intense and long-lasting loyalties to one's party were no longer what they seemed to be becoming in Jefferson's time. But politics had not been placid throughout the eight years of Jackson's presidency. National interest quickened, organization developed to keep pace, and partisan loyalties grew and deepened. But these were far from well established or as yet the norm of American politics as Jackson approached retirement.

Jackson's strong policies and advocacy, his determination to have his own way in politics and policy leadership had caused the rise of a determined opposition intent on doing away with Jackson's men and their program. In the aftermath of the bitter war over the recharter of the Bank of the United States in 1833–1834, this opposition had hardened sufficiently in every state to pose a formidable resistance to the dominant Democrats. Indeed, the electorate seemed very closely divided. In the off years elections in 1834 and 1835 the emerging Whigs had gained significantly over their poor showing against Jackson only two years earlier. In a number of states they turned lopsided Democratic presidential margins into Whig governorships, Whig-controlled legislatures, and made important additions to Whig congressional strength.[4]

In the face of this rising opposition, the ruling Democrats had a critical problem. They had to contest the upcoming presidential election without Andrew Jackson, their popular standard bearer. His closest adviser and heir apparent, Martin Van Buren, had no popular aura or appeal of his own, and was unlikely to attract the kind of lionization Jackson had received from voters. But the Democrats believed that they still had an ideological majority in the country—that most people supported their policy stances.

[4] There is an excellent state by state survey of these developments in McCormick, *Second American Party System.*

That support had to be mobilized, however, and made to realize what was at stake. It could not be distracted by false matters or concern for personalities. To accomplish this, the Democrats dramatically struck out in new directions with far-reaching consequences for the future course of American politics.

At the centerpiece of their efforts was the political party. A number of Jackson's colleagues had early argued that in an era of increasing popular participation in politics over an extended geographic area some kind of disciplined and united national organization was necessary to organize the electorate, select candidates, provide policy direction to the faithful, mute internal differences and develop the means of achieving the fullest measure of popular support.[5] The crucial underpinning of this organization was its motivating philosophy expressing unity of principles and singleness of purpose against its adversaries. "Union, harmony, self-denial, concession, everything for the cause, nothing for men . . ." was the way one Democratic congressman expressed it early in the campaign.[6] More than anything else, jealousies, indifference, or internal squabbles over candidates had to be prevented. Otherwise the party would fail and its principles be defeated. There were real differences between the parties, they argued, and the stakes in the upcoming election were clear enough. The Whigs wished to re-establish "that train of measures introduced by the administration of John Quincy Adams": the Bank, a system of federal internal improvements, a corrupt land policy, and a

[5] There are excellent analyses of the attitudes toward and the role of parties in this period in Michael Wallace, "Changing Concepts of Party in the United States: New York, 1815–1825," *Amer. Hist. Rev.* 74, (December, 1968): pp. 453–491; Roy F. Nichols, *The Invention of American Political Parties* (New York, 1967); Perry Goldman, "Political Virtue in the Age of Jackson," *Polit. Sci. Quart.* 87 (March, 1972) : pp. 46–62.

[6] The remark was made by Cave Johnson and is quoted in Clement L. Grant, "The Public Career of Cave Johnson" (Ph.D., Vanderbilt University, 1951), p. 80.

high tariff, all of which would destroy the prosperity and the freedom of the people of the United States so long basking in the virtues of Democratic principles. Any Democrat, no matter who he was, could be relied on to counter this in the name of Democratic policies. "If Van Buren be the rallying point of anti-bankism, antinullification, what republicans will fail to rally around him? Is his mere name to frighten men from their principles . . . ?"[7] The relationship between the two was never forgotten.

Holding a national convention was not altogether new but was certainly unusual in 1836. Several had been held four years before but most nominations in the early 1830's continued to be a haphazard affair of local and caucus nominations or legislative endorsements. This now changed. The second national Democratic nominating convention met in Baltimore in May, 1835. The whole meeting was deliberately orchestrated as a grand rally of the party faithful, to reaffirm party principles and pass the leadership mantle to Martin Van Buren. It unanimously nominated him, as "the executor of [Jacksonian] principles," whose election would "preserve the power of our party and secure the triumph of his [Jackson's] principles."[8] The second spot was given to Richard M. Johnson of Kentucky, another stalwart party man. Finally, the convention issued an elaborate statement of party ideology—a quasi-platform—to publicize and underscore the Democratic stance and Van Buren's place in it.[9] Everything that the Democrats did in the campaign followed this basic strategy of recalling all Democrats to their duty behind Van Buren to preserve what had been gained.

[7] Washington *Globe*, March 19, 1835.
[8] Milledgeville (Ga.) *Federal Union*, April 21, 1835, January 18, 1836.
[9] The Democrats' "Address to the People" ran in most Democratic newspapers. It is reprinted in Silbey, "Election of 1836," pp. 616–638.

In contrast to their adversaries, the Whigs in 1836 were not nearly as well organized. Still in their shaking-down phase as a party with several different power blocs in often uneasy alliance with one another, they had not as yet developed any deep sense of party attachment or loyalty out of which could grow harmony, concert, and a spirit of compromise. They were particularly deeply divided over who should be their candidate. Whig newspaper editorials were filled with hopes for harmony on a single ticket and their acute consciousness that they probably could not achieve it.[10] A national convention would only underscore these divisions. They relied instead on the traditional way to bring forward their candidates. Informal legislative caucuses, local meetings, and conventions in different states named Hugh L. White, Daniel Webster, and William Henry Harrison for the presidency.

A number of Whig leaders perceived in their lack of organization a means towards overcoming the hated Democrats. First, they appealed to the localism still rampant in American politics. White would run in the South, Webster in New England, Harrison in the West, each to appeal to particular local prejudices or the attractiveness of one or another candidate. Nicholas Biddle articulated this well. "I have said again and again to my friends," he wrote, "this disease is to be treated as a local disorder—apply local remedies." [11]

To further this, they would also run a campaign, particularly in the strong Democratic areas, de-emphasizing party identification and appealing to potential dissident Democrats to break the shackles of party discipline for other goals. At the core of their strategy as it developed,

---

[10] See, for example, the Washington *National Intelligencer,* July 1, 1835.
[11] Nicholas Biddle to Herman Cope, August 11, 1835, in Reginald McGrane (ed.), *The Correspondence of Nicholas Biddle Dealing With National Affairs, 1807–1844* (Boston, 1919), p. 255.

therefore, was a full-scale attack on party organization, discipline, and loyalty as reprehensible and subversive of American institutions.[12]

"Party division," the Cincinnati *Daily Gazette* wrote, "is an unhealthy and unsafe condition of things. Its tendency is to substitute mere party objects and coercive party discipline for the exercise of sound discretion in deciding upon measures." That had happened under Jackson. The government was now "administered for the Party—not for the People." But, "the watchword of every American," an Indiana Whig meeting resolved, "should be 'our country,' not 'our Party.'" The Whig's particular target was, of course, Martin Van Buren, the organizer of party institutions, and the "little magician" of American politics. "The Vice-President, thro' the Kitchen Cabinet has supplanted most of the early friends of the President, and has succeeded in establishing at Washington, the discipline of the New York school of politics." [13]

Finally, the Whigs attempted to take advantage of local prejudices and fears by explicitly denying the ability of national organizations to solve pressing local or sectional problems. A particular laboratory of this Whig strategy was the South, acutely sensitive as many there were to the recent rise of abolitionist activities in the North. The abolitionists' incessant pamphleteering and propagandizing against slavery had provoked a furor in the Southern States. Several slave state legislatures passed strong anti-abolitionist resolutions warning against the consequences of further agitation and of any implicit or explicit Northern support

12 See the speech of Congressman John Bell in Nashville, Tennessee, July, 1835, reprinted in Silbey, "Election of 1836," p. 639.

13 Cincinnati *Daily Gazette*, reprinted in *National Intelligencer*, August 1, 1835. See also, Albany *Evening Journal*, February 10, 1836; *National Intelligencer*, September 30, 1835. The attack on Van Buren is from Albany *Evening Journal*, March 19, 1835.

of their activities.[14]   It was this mood that Southern Whigs endeavored to exploit against Van Buren.

Their candidate in most Southern States was shrewdly chosen.   Hugh Lawson White was an original supporter of Jackson who had angrily left the party during the Bank war.   The Whigs emphasized first that he remained a loyal Jacksonian devoted to the original principles of the party now corrupted.   And they particularly stressed that he was a Southerner and therefore sensitive to Southern values and needs.[15]

They directed their arguments against the Southern supporters of the Democratic ticket who, controlled by a "base party spirit," were playing down sectional differences and the danger to the South.   If such men would forget political parties, the South might still be saved, for its only hope was political unity.   The South "must *organize*. The South must concentrate.   Upon this subject there is no room for party." [16]   They must do so, finally, behind a Southern candidate.   In the North, "those who favor abolition outnumber those who do not."   The Northerners would therefore soon demand action by the federal government against the South's peculiar institution, and any Northern politician, including the president, whatever his inclinations, would have to succumb to the pressure and ultimately advocate or execute hostile actions against slavery.   "Vote for a Northern President from a free state," a Virginia newspaper warned, "and when the test comes,

[14] There are samplings of these reprinted in State of New York, *Messages From the Governors* (Albany, 1909) 3: pp. 582n–583n, 588.   See also, the resolutions of a public meeting in South Carolina in late 1835, reprinted in *Niles Register,* October 3, 1835.

[15] White's career is ably traced in Lunia Paul Gresham, "The Public Career of Hugh Lawson White" (Ph.D., Vanderbilt University, 1943).   There is a wealth of documentary material in Nancy N. Scott (ed.), *A Memoir of Hugh Lawson White* (Philadelphia, 1856).

[16] Richmond *Whig,* May 18, 1835; Washington *United States Telegraph,* October 26, 1835.

he will support the abolitionists.[17]   They also pointed to the Democrats' nomination of Johnson, who had lived with a black woman for many years, as indicative of the Jacksonians' indifference to and lack of sensitivity about Southern values.[18]

Elsewhere, where it suited them, that is in strong Whig areas, the Whigs were not hesitant to stand firmly against Democratic policies on ideological grounds, and to pose their own alternatives.[19]   But the main thrust of their campaign was clear enough: to challenge the organizational revolution on which the Democrats relied in order to blur and weaken party lines and to exploit Democratic candidate weaknesses and local prejudices.

The Democratic response to this was clear and crisp. In the South they deprecated sectionalism as dangerous and inappropriate since there was a "total want of any real ground of dissension between the North and the South," attacked the Whigs for raising the issue, the only means they had "of inflaming the passion of the people, so prosperous and happy are they under the administration of Andrew Jackson" and particularly defended Van Buren from the assaults leveled against him.[20] He was "emphatically a FIRM FRIEND OF THE SOUTH." His past record and particularly his votes are "no violation of

[17] Quoted in Henry Simms, *The Rise of the Whigs in Virginia* (Richmond, 1929), p. 100.

[18] "It may be a matter of no importance to mere political automatons whether Richard M. Johnson is a *white* or a *black* man," a Whig newspaper argued. "Whether he is *free* or slave—or whether he is married to, or has been in connection with a jet-black, thick lipped, oderiferous negro wench" but to the South it did. *United States Telegraph*, June 3, 1835. At their state convention in mid-1836, Virginia Democrats nominated William Smith instead of Johnson for the vice-presidency.

[19] See the exchange of letters between Sherrod Williams and General William Henry Harrison in April and May, 1836, reprinted in Silbey, "Election of 1836," pp. 607–613. Harrison's statements were widely circulated among the Whig faithful.

[20] Washington *Globe*, May 5, 1835; *Federal Union*, March 11, 18, 1836; *Richmond Enquirer*, June 30, 1835, January 19, March 15, April 15, 1836.

the rights of the South, no interference with the interests of the South, no evidence of hostility to the welfare of the South."[21]   Most of all, however, as they had done everywhere throughout the campaign, they redoubled their emphasis on party and partisanship and attacked the Whigs' blurring of their ideological differences.   Once more they reiterated the familiar refrain: "if bankism, nullification, anti-instructionism, anti-Jacksonianism, and everything that is anti-republican, rallies under the White flag, and Van Burenism be the opposite, who should hesitate to give a preference to Van Buren? *Principles are everything; men nothing.*"[22]   In sum, as Thomas Ritchie wrote, "the true issue is between Van Buren and Harrison—the Democratic opinions of one and the Federal opinions of the other."[23]

There was in all of this a good deal of cool calculation and careful assessment by both parties.   The Whigs, faced with the need to overcome a national majority party, primarily pursued a minority party strategy, searching for the best means of splitting some voters away from their normal moorings by fuzzing the lines between them, by supporting a proto-Democrat and by stressing some crucial issue of a non-partisan character.   The Democrats had countered all of this by running a national campaign, relying on their organization and the loyalties of their supporters, by distinctly drawing party and policy lines between themselves and the opposition, reminding their adherents why they were Democrats in the first place and why they should remain so, and parrying and exposing all of the subterfuges of the opposition.

In all that they were doing in the campaign, both parties were implanting an essential structure into the

---

[21] *Federal Union*, April 8, June 16, 1836.
[22] Washington *Globe*, June 27, 1835.
[23] *Richmond Enquirer*, March 29, 1836.

American election style unlike anything yet seen. In calling on their organizational strength and loyalties as they did the Democrats were bidding for a discipline from the electorate unlike anything yet sought. The Democratic party had matured greatly as an organization during the campaign, the Whigs were beginning to adopt many of the same rules.

Both parties campaigned hard. They set up local and state committees, organized fund-raising activities, held local and state conventions, established newspapers and coordinated their activities through state central committees. Newspaper editorials from the party press, extensive pamphleteering, and campaign biographies set the tone; rallies, barbecues, dinners, stump speeches and debates followed as part and parcel of the American campaign style. Local addresses to the people, similar to that issued nationally, appeared. Even the presidential candidates themselves toured somewhat to attend the rallies and dinners in their behalf. Harrison did the most, going to New York, Pennsylvania, and Virginia at one point or another in the race. If the amount of activity did not quite reach the level or intensity of later years, it was substantial for its time.[24] Certainly it went beyond anything yet known, in keeping with the whole thrust of the campaign. Neither party was more passive than the other. If the Whigs' efforts were imperfect, this reflected more their late development than any lack of will. Where they had been active for some time, they made use of existing party organizational techniques as well as the Democrats did. Certainly they engaged in elaborate, and successful, attempts at coordinating their ticket. Harrison was on the ballot in fifteen states, Webster only in New England,

[24] Charles Grier Sellers, Jr., *James K. Polk, Jacksonian 1795–1843* (Princeton, 1957), chap. 8–9, has an excellent description of one congressman's rather extensive activities in this campaign.

White in ten states, mostly slaveholding. There had been much maneuvering and agreements among the Whigs to effect this. The Virginia Harrison convention met and adopted the ticket of electors selected earlier by the White forces there, so that the same electors would be chosen regardless of which candidate an individual Whig preferred.[25] In no place was more than one set of Whig electors on the ballot, so despite their plethora of candidates the Whigs did make it a two-party race in every state. In sum, as one Virginian wrote to Van Buren late in the campaign, "parties have never been so thoroughly organized in Virginia as now, and I am happy to tell you that the Republicans are not outdone by their adversaries."[26]

As the campaign itself had advanced one set of critical elements in American politics, the results of the election underscored another. Popular participation increased only slightly over what it had been four years earlier, but voter turnout soared in most southern States and a few others.[27] This indication of the quickening of interest and the bitterness of the campaign was also reflected in the actual voting returns. The pattern of voting in recent presidential elections had been noteworthy, first for the large margins between the parties. In both 1828 and 1832 Jackson had won with around 55 per cent of the total vote. Even more noteworthy, each party's support was highly local and sectional in nature. Most sections of the country and most states were solidly committed to one or the other party. The Democrats, for example, received 83 per cent of the popular vote in the South Atlantic States in 1828, and 63 per cent in the Southwest. Some of their margins in in-

25 The Virginia situation is described in Simms, *Rise of the Virginia Whigs*, pp. 108–109.

26 William C. Rives to Martin Van Buren, October 13, 1836, Martin Van Buren Papers, Library of Congress.

27 The turnout figures were originally computed by Richard McCormick. See his "New Perspectives on Jacksonian Politics," *Amer. Hist. Rev.* **65** (January, 1960): pp. 288–301.

dividual states were enormous. Jackson had received over 95 per cent of the popular vote in Georgia and Tennessee, and 67 per cent in Illinois. On the other hand, he had received only one-quarter of the vote in several of the New England States. In 1828 there were eight states where the differences between the candidates were 50 per cent or more—meaning that one party was getting more than three-quarters of the popular vote. Four years later, the number of such states had been reduced by two but there were six others where one party received 60 per cent or more of the popular vote. In other words, in half the states in 1832, there were essentially one-party systems, only two less than in 1828. Only in the Middle Atlantic States of New York and New Jersey in both elections, Maryland, Louisiana, Maine, New Hampshire, and Ohio in 1828, and Delaware in 1832 was there close to an even break in the vote.[28]

In 1836 all of this dramatically changed. There was a major reshuffling of voter preferences between the two parties (table 1). The bitter political events of the past eight years, the disappearance of the charismatic Jackson and the intense upbeat in party organization and campaign techniques all now produced a new political and electoral configuration. First of all, in contrast to recent contests, the election was remarkably close. Van Buren garnered only 50.9 per cent of the popular vote. (In fact the defection of Virginia's Democratic electors forced the election of the vice-president into the Senate.) The close results also reflected something else: the geography of American politics had significantly changed. In most of the previously one-sided states, there were wide swings from one party to the other. The Democrats lost heavily in both the

[28] All election figures are drawn from Walter Dean Burnham, *Presidential Ballots, 1836–1892* (Baltimore, 1955); and Sven Peterson, *A Statistical History of American Presidential Elections* (New York, 1963).

TABLE 1

DEMOCRATIC VOTE BY SECTION
1832–1836

	1832	1836	Change
New England	39.8%	51.4%	+11.6%
Middle Atlantic	54.4	53.0	− 1.4
Border	49.9	46.0	− 3.9
South Atlantic	83.2	52.7	−30.5
Southwest	62.9	49.2	−13.7
[Slave South]	67.8	50.0	−17.8
Old Northwest	55.5	48.6	− 6.9

South and West. In the slave states Van Buren dropped 18 per cent below Jackson's figure four years before. In five states the shift in the popular vote exceeded 30 per cent between the two elections, including two where the change exceeded 50 per cent, and two others, where the shift from one party to the other since 1832 was more than 40 per cent. Everywhere in the South there was now enormous Whig strength. In Tennessee, for instance, the largest voter shift in the whole country occurred. It had been one of Jackson's bellwether states in 1828 and 1832, giving him over 95 per cent of its vote each time. Now it went Whig.

In the rest of the country, there were similar shifts. In Massachusetts, despite the favorite-son candidacy of Daniel Webster on behalf of the Whigs, the Democrats gained 21 per cent over their margin in 1832 rising to 45 per cent of the popular vote. In three other states they gained at least 15 per cent. In the West, similar overturns occurred. In Illinois, the Whigs increased their share of the presidential vote by 17 percentage points, and picked up many local officers for the first time. Abraham Lincoln was elected in the state legislature in a district in which the Democratic vote had remained largely stable since 1832 but where the Whig vote had doubled in the same period. Only in the Middle Atlantic States, already closely com-

TABLE 2

A.

States in which the Democrats increased their percentage of the popular vote over 1832:

Massachusetts	+21.7
New Hampshire	+17.7
Connecticut	+15.8
Rhode Island	+15.7
Vermont	+15.6
Maine	+ 5.3
New York	+ 2.5
Kentucky	+ 2.0

B.

States in which the Whigs increased their percentage of the popular vote over 1832:

Tennessee	+53.4
Georgia	+52.7
Mississippi	+49.3
Missouri	+40.0
North Carolina	+31.2
Indiana	+23.1
Virginia	+17.7
Illinois	+17.6
Louisiana	+ 9.7
Pennsylvania	+ 6.5
Maryland	+ 3.8
Ohio	+ 3.4
Delaware	+ 2.8
New Jersey	+ 0.5

petitive between the parties, was there little change in voting patterns since 1832 (table 2).[29]

Each party became nationwide in scope as each penetrated deeply into the bailiwicks of the other. In every

29 A political scientist, Gerald Pomper, has correlated the distribution of the popular vote in 1836 with the distribution in earlier elections. If the voting groups within each party had remained stable as they usually do between two adjoining elections, the correlation figure between the two would be relatively high. The voting patterns in 1828 correlated with those of 1832 at a figure of .93, for example, a very high correlation. But the pattern in 1836 was only slightly correlated with either 1828 or 1832. The correlation between 1836 and 1828 was .05, between 1836 and 1832, .22. See Gerald Pomper, *Elections In America* (New York, 1968), p. 268.

region and almost every state, there were now quite close divisions between Whigs and Democrats. In 1832 Jackson beat Clay by a two to one margin in eleven states, but in 1836, only one state, New Hampshire, where Van Buren received 75 per cent of the vote, remained in that distended category. In three states, Connecticut, Mississippi, and New Jersey, the difference between the two parties was less than one per cent; in five more, the difference between them was 5 per cent or less. In fourteen states in all, (with a majority in the electoral college), the minority party received at least 45 per cent of the popular vote and could be said to be very competitive with the other party, i.e., the state could go either way in a presidential election, a significant change from the recent past. In 1832, by comparison, only seven states had been competitive.

A deeply divided and highly competitive partisan electorate had emerged in 1836. Neither party any longer enjoyed the luxury of safe states or regions. For the first time in our history a truly national two-party vote existed. Nor were these patterns transient. In state after state the voting patterns articulated in 1836 set and hardened into permanence. In most elections, thereafter, the dominant mood of the electorate was for continuity and stability. Most of the time, the same groups continued to support the same parties despite the rise of new issues, or charismatic candidates or the intensity of internal divisions. There was no major reshuffling of votes similar to 1836 for twenty years, longer than that in many areas. As a result each party's total vote moved through a very narrow band and national elections remained close and fiercely competitive.[30]

On a scale of dramatic events, hyperbolic rhetoric and colorful personalities, perhaps 1836 does deserve low marks

[30] Elections were quite close nationally and in most states in the succeeding twenty years. The correlations between each party's vote in these same elections were very high, i.e., the same groups continued to support the same party in each election.

for its grayness to the contemporary observer. On the other hand, few elections have had such importance in revealing and articulating the underlying currents and trends of national politics. The celebration of party and not personality by the Democrats and their heavy emphasis on ideology had both contributed to the establishment of a new climate in the American political culture. The redistribution of the vote and the locking of voters into their party homes had also made an important mark. The Whigs were most unhappy about their narrow defeat but they had learned something from the Democrats. "There was a general waking up to the conviction," Horace Greeley remembered, that Van Buren "might have been beaten *by seasonable concert and effort.*" Particularly, Henry Clay felt, they had failed because "no mode was devised and none seemed practicable to present a single candidate in opposition." [31] But from now on they would have a national convention and agreement on a single popular candidate to add to their commitment to electioneering, articulated campaign strategies, and all else implied in the new politics of the mid-thirties.

There was no turning back. The election of 1840 completed the process begun in 1836. Nineteenth-century and much of twentieth-century American politics was dominated by party organization, party discipline, and deeply ingrained voter loyalties to their parties, rarely to men. All of these things had been in the making particularly in the years after 1815. The election of 1836 gave them extraordinary impetus and remains therefore second to few as a defining point in American political life.

JOEL H. SILBEY
Professor of American History,
Cornell University

---

[31] Horace Greeley, *Recollections of A Busy Life* (New York, 1868), p. 113; Henry Clay to Hugh Lawson White, August 27, 1838, in *Memoir of White*, p. 367.

The Election of 1860

I N 1860, the presidential race should have been a close one between Stephen A. Douglas of Illinois and William H. Seward of New York, with some lesser competition from remnants of the Whig and American parties. If Douglas had won, there probably would have been no secession; if Seward had won, there probably would have been no firing on Fort Sumter. Instead, a majority of Republicans in convention rejected Seward and nominated Abraham Lincoln, while a large minority of Democrats, mostly southerners, rejected Douglas and split their party. Lincoln, less handicapped than Seward by the stigma of radicalism, won an election that the New Yorker might have lost. The deep South, to whom all Republicans looked alike, rejected Lincoln as president and seceded from the Union. Lincoln and other Republican leaders rejected compromise while also refusing to acquiesce in peaceable separation. And the war came.

Of all American presidential elections, that of 1860 is the one that most obviously qualifies as "crucial." Indeed, it might well be regarded as a model of crucial elections, except that in some ways and especially in its aftermath, the election of 1860 was unique. If a crucial election is a contest that leads directly to disunion and civil war, there has been only one such phenomenon in American history— a phenomenon full of its own special drama and meaning, but not lending itself readily to analogy or comparative analysis. So perhaps it would be more useful to say that this was one of a number of elections that may be labeled *crucial* but the only one that proved to be *catastrophic*. The distinction is important because it is one thing to study the election of 1860 as an example of a critical election and something else again to study it as the immediate cause of the Civil War. But if we begin by identifying the elements of cruciality that it shares with certain other presidential campaigns, it may then be easier to recognize the influences uniquely linking this election with catastrophe.

Of course the meaning and importance of an election may vary considerably according to the angle of observation. For American Catholics, the presidential campaigns of 1928 and 1960 had special significance. For American Negroes, those famous pivotal contests of 1800 and 1828 were virtually meaningless, whereas the election of 1868 was perhaps crucial. The fundamental distinction, however, is between the contemporary view and the retrospective one. To participants, a crucial election is one that offers a relatively clear choice on matters of supreme importance; to historians, it is one that had notable consequences or marked a sharp turn in the course of events. These do not necessarily amount to the same thing. For example, voters in 1932 had more of a choice, and voters in 1964 had less of a choice, than they realized at the time. But concerning the election of 1860 there appears to be no doubt. From almost every point of view it was a crucial election, recognized as such by contemporaries and confirmed as such by successive generations of historians. The angle of observation may affect its meaning but cannot diminish its importance.

If the election of 1932 seemed crucial at the time, it was because of the historical context rather than the range of choice apparently offered by the contestants. Not until four years later did the electorate have an opportunity to pass judgment on the New Deal. An election held in critical times is to some extent a crucial one *ipso facto,* no matter who the candidates may be; for a crisis can magnify the effect of minor differences.   For example, the campaign of 1848 took place during a four-year sectional crisis over slavery, but its two major candidates offered voters such a blurred choice that they divided both the North and South rather equally between them.   By 1850, however, the difference between Zachary Taylor and Lewis Cass was enough to have perhaps provoked the Civil War ten years ahead of time, if death had not auspiciously intervened.

In the case of 1860, to be sure, crisis is equated with the secession movement that followed the election.   There is not enough recognition of the extent to which the entire contest was conducted in an atmosphere of crisis.   John Brown's grave was still new when the national conventions assembled in the spring, and rumors of incipient slave uprisings, supposedly plotted by itinerant abolitionist agents, continued to ripple through the southern states.   Fear that a Lincoln victory might inspire re-enactment of "the horrors of St. Domingo" was expressed privately on the eve of the election by no less a personage than the chief justice of the United States.[1]

A slave-revolt panic had also struck the South four years earlier, and in several other ways the elections of 1856 and 1860 were remarkably similar.   Voters in each instance had a relatively clear and decisive choice on the same paramount issue.   Party alignments were much alike, except for Democratic unity in 1856 and division in 1860. Civil war in Kansas provided a background of crisis in 1856, and fear of a Republican victory inspired the southern threats of secession that were to be heard again in 1860. The outcome, of course, was different in 1856.   Instead of escalating the sectional crisis, it evoked the loudest sighs of relief since the success of compromise in 1850.   But does the different outcome exclude the campaign of 1856 from

[1] Roger B. Taney to J. Mason Campbell, October 19, 1860, Benjamin C. Howard Papers, Maryland Historical Society.

the category of crucial elections? Was it any less critical than the campaign of 1860? There is a parallel in the elections of 1796 and 1800, which presented similar issues and the same presidential candidates, but had different results. The choices, potentialities, and hazards were much the same on both occasions; yet only the victory of Jefferson over Adams is ordinarily labeled "crucial."

Obviously, we have come up against a definitional problem. Does cruciality inhere primarily in choices offered or in decisions taken, in the alternatives or the consequences? And further, is a decision to embrace change or initiate action more "crucial" than a decision to reject change or refrain from acting? The standard attitude of American historians seems well illustrated in their treatment of these two pairs of elections, 1796–1800 and 1856–1860. The decision is what counts, but a negative decision does not count very much.

If so, however, then what about the election of 1896? Here, as in 1796 and 1856, the alternatives overshadow the outcome, and who lost seems more important than who won. Yet historians commonly regard the McKinley-Bryan contest as "crucial." In some significant way, it must resemble the elections of 1800 and 1860, but how? Let us imagine that a suicidal young man named John Doe goes to a tenth-floor window, climbs out on the ledge, thinks about it, and climbs back inside. Later, he goes to the same window, climbs out on the ledge, and jumps. Which was the more crucial decision? Before replying, you should of course ask, "How *much* later?" If it was an hour, a month, or even a year, the right answer is no doubt "the decision to jump." But what if the interval was thirty or forty years, during which time Mr. Doe became a famous author, a millionaire, and a two-handicap golfer, with a beautiful, passionate wife and six gifted, non-rebellious children? The effective duration of a decision may largely determine just how crucial it was. The elections of 1796 and 1856 were both reversed four years later. The election of 1896, on the other hand, produced a decision that lasted. Like the campaigns of 1800 and 1860, it ushered in an identifiable historical period of some duration.

In addition, the McKinley-Bryan contest is one of the presidential campaigns that have acquired transcendant meaning as embodiments of the elemental and everlasting clash between democracy and privilege. Bryan, the "great commoner," became a major figure in America's democratic mythology, along with Jefferson, Jackson, Wilson, and Franklin Roosevelt. But the election of 1860 was no classic confrontation of classes, and the victor differed from those five leaders in his party allegiance. There is no reason why the greatest human symbol of democracy should have been a Whig-turned-Republican or why he should have emerged in the year 1860—no reason, that is, save the unique personality and genius of Abraham Lincoln. Still, symbolic heroes and crucial elections seem to go together, perhaps because historians put them together, and the election of 1860 is no exception.

There *is* a conspicuous exception, however, which poses another terminological question. The heroic figure of George Washington is not associated with a "crucial" election. Yet the office of the presidency was virtually tailored to fit this man, and in certain respects, no other election was as important—indeed, as *necessary*—as his in 1789. But of course it was also a foregone conclusion. No one else received any electoral votes in 1789 or in 1792. The question is, how close must an election be to qualify as "crucial"? Can a mismatch such as that of 1936 (Roosevelt, 532 electoral votes; Landon, 8) be called "crucial," even taking into account the false expectations aroused by the *Literary Digest?* The answer, I suspect, is that a lop-sided score does not necessarily make a contest less critical—not, for instance, if it is the seventh game of the World Series. Nevertheless, in popular thought at least, a crucial election must be in some way a historical forking-point. This means that in retrospect it probably must be a contest that might easily have had a different outcome—such as an election of 1884 without its Reverend Samuel D. Burchard.[2] The conception of what is "crucial" usually includes some elements of contingency and choice, even of horseshoe-nail causality. It is extremely difficult to associate cruciality with inevitability.

Since hope springs eternal, an election more often seems close in prospect than in retrospect. It is not customary to acknowledge even the possibility of defeat, and only once in American history has the outcome of a relatively close election been openly predicted months ahead of time, not only by the winners but by many of the losers. Lincoln won the presidency in 1860 by converting a mere 39 per cent of the popular vote into 59 per cent of the electoral vote. Some modest changes in a few strategic places would have produced a different result. Yet by midsummer numerous Americans were echoing John D. Ashmore of South Carolina in his assertion that Lincoln's election was "almost certain." [3]

There were several influences contributing to this anomaly. First, the division of the opposition meant that no other candidate could possibly win in the electoral college. The only real alternative to a Lincoln victory was an election thrown into the House of Representatives, where the Republicans might have some trouble piecing out a majority. Thus the choice offered voters was simply

2 In 1884 James G. Blaine lost New York and the presidency to Grover Cleveland by only 1,149 votes. Burchard, in Blaine's presence, angered Catholics by referring to Democrats as the party of "Rum, Romanism and Rebellion."

3 Ollinger Crenshaw, *The Slave States in the Presidential Election of 1860* (Baltimore, 1945), p. 211.

"yes" or "no" on Lincoln, without any assurance that a "no" vote would stick.[4] Furthermore, the sectional commitments were so firmly set in most parts of the country that the decision actually rested with a trio of pivotal states —Pennsylvania, Indiana, and Illinois—all of which had recorded strong shifts toward Republicanism. And finally, southern fire-eaters loudly predicted a Lincoln victory in order to encourage preparations for secession.

Thus, in spite of all the oratory and pageantry, the election of 1860 was not in itself a suspenseful contest. The tension mounting day by day resulted much less from uncertainty about the outcome than from anxiety about the expected sequel. Any lingering doubt was dissolved in October when Republican candidates won the state elections in Pennsylvania and Indiana. Even Stephen A. Douglas acknowledged defeat at this point. "Mr. Lincoln is the next President," he declared. "We must try to save the Union." [5] This, mind you, was a month before the presidential election. We tend to think of a crucial campaign as one in which there is considerable doubt about the outcome, but here there was an unusual degree of certitude about the outcome long before the votes were counted, and this certitude may have turned a crisis into a catastrophe.

The presidential election of 1860 was by no means the only one to precipitate a crisis. The years 1800 and 1876 immediately spring to mind. However, both of those

---

[4] Out of 33 votes in a House election, Republicans were sure of only 15, but there was reason to believe that some northern Democratic congressmen would vote for Lincoln if Douglas was not in the contest. One remote southern hope was that no candidate would be able to get a majority in the House, whereupon the duties of the presidency would devolve upon the new vice president chosen by the Senate. That would almost certainly be the candidate of the southern Democrats, Joseph Lane of Oregon (running-mate of John C. Breckinridge). See *ibid.*, pp. 61–73; Roy Franklin Nichols, *The Disruption of American Democracy* (New York, 1948), pp. 338–339.

[5] George Fort Milton, *The Eve of Conflict: Stephen A. Douglas and the Needless War* (Boston, 1934), p. 496.

crises were caused by the abnormal inconclusiveness of the election results—in sharp contrast with the grim certainty of Lincoln's victory.   Neither was the campaign of 1860 unique in reflecting a bitter sectional cleavage in national politics; for as far back as 1796 the election of John Adams had constituted a triumph of North over South.   Only in 1860, however, did a large bloc of states fail to give the winning candidate a single popular vote.[6]   And although the two-party system has certainly broken down at other times, only in 1860 do we find the oddity of virtually two separate presidential races (Lincoln vs. Douglas in the North and Bell vs. Breckinridge in the South), one of which was more or less inconsequential.   Furthermore, Lincoln was not the first president-elect to be regarded as in league with the Devil, but whereas certain New England ladies in 1801, for instance, allegedly feared that Thomas Jefferson would confiscate their Bibles, many southerners in 1860 feared that Lincoln would subvert their slaves and thus put their very lives in danger.

Of course these and other peculiar characteristics setting the election of 1860 apart from other presidential campaigns were to some extent merely symptoms of the sectional conflict.   Indeed, it is difficult to ignore an impression that the voters in 1860 were essentially acting out a decision already firmly made.   One leading dictionary defines "crucial" as "involving a final and supreme decision," but in history as in a bureaucracy, the final decision may not be the truly effective one.   In the drama called "The Coming of the Civil War," the election of 1860 often seems to be more a part of the dénouement than a part of the climax.   So many options had already been closed off by the late 1850's that there may have been no forking-point left with a path leading directly away from disaster.

---

[6] In the eleven states that eventually constituted the Confederacy, Lincoln received only about 2,000 votes, all in Virginia.

A Republican failure to capture the presidency in 1860 would probably have meant skirting the precipice for another four years. In contrast, the campaign of 1844 can be pointed to as a real forking-point; for the nomination of Van Buren instead of Polk or the election of Clay instead of Polk would have changed the whole timetable of history by preventing, moderating, or at least delaying the territorial expansion that revived the sectional quarrel over slavery.

If alternatives were limited in 1860 because of decisions reached in earlier elections, they were even more profoundly affected by decisions made less formally and more gradually outside the electoral process. I refer especially to the development of the southern conviction that slavery must be protected at all costs, to the diverging sectional beliefs about the value and sanctity of the Union, and to the hardening opinion of a northern majority that slavery was incompatible with the destinies of the Republic. These were the fundamental decisions acted out in the election of 1860 and in its aftermath of secession and civil war.

Thus the election itself may be viewed as a terminal symptom, the study of which only scratches the surface of the problem of war causation that has so fascinated historians. Yet one wonders how often in history rebellions and other such cataclysmic events do *not* occur, even in the presence of adequate causes, simply because there is no practical point of impulse where feeling and belief can be translated into action. The record of sectional confrontations dating back to the 1790's made it abundantly clear that no common interest—not even the defense of slavery—could induce the South to act as a unit. Fire-eaters lived with the memory of the cold reception given the Virginia and Kentucky resolutions in other southern states, of South Carolina out on its lonely limb in 1833, of Southern congressmen refusing to sign Calhoun's "Southern Address," of the abortive efforts to launch a secession movement in 1851. But then, complete unity was not necessary, for if a respectable number of states were to act in concert, the rest of the South would probably follow. The problem of secessionists in these first-line states, stretching around the coast from the Carolinas to Texas, was not so much to arouse sentiment as to crystallize initiative.

In the past, southern disaffection had usually been inspired by proceedings of Congress, such as enactment of a tariff measure in 1832 and introduction of the Wilmot Proviso in 1846. But Congress was a place where half loaves were common fare, and in each instance the crisis had been defused by compromise or something resembling compromise. This had happened as recently as 1858, when the so-called "English bill" put an end to the fierce Lecompton controversy. Two years earlier, however, the presidential election had for the first time become a potential signal of disunion, and by 1860 it was evident that a Lincoln victory would have a more explosive effect than any legislative proposals likely to receive serious attention from Congress in the immediate future. The Buchanan administration had in fact managed to sweep the dangerous territorial issue somewhat messily under the rug, but, ironically, it had done so in a manner that enhanced Republican chances of capturing the presidency. This meant that a different finger was now on the trigger. Control had shifted from the professional politician to the ordinary voter, particularly the northern voter. Moreover, an election, unlike an act of Congress, is a fixed target date on the calendar, and its results cannot be reshaped by last-minute compromise.

For the fundamental causes of the Civil War we should have to look much deeper into American history, but if we are just trying to understand why the final crisis came about when it did and took the form that it did, then the campaign of 1860 and the electoral process as a whole deserve close attention. Consider, for instance, the effect of Lincoln's nomination over Seward, which may well have made the difference between victory and defeat for the Republicans; or the influence of the general-ticket system in the choice of electors, which enabled a man to become president against the wishes of three-fifths of the voters.

Most important of all, perhaps, were those conditions and arrangements that made the presidential election a long-awaited signal for rebellion and that allowed secession to proceeed so far without resistance. They include the four-month interval between election day and inauguration day, a constitutional relic foolishly retained in the era of the railroad and telegraph; also, those October state elections that confirmed southern apprehensions a month ahead of time; and above all, those peculiar circumstances that caused a relatively close election to be regarded far in advance as virtually a foregone conclusion. For a moment, imagine Lincoln winning instead an election that was in doubt all the way—better still, an election thrown into the House of Representatives. Would southerners, hopeful to the last, have been able then to launch a successful disunion movement? It seems unlikely. The pall of inevitability hanging over the campaign (which sets it apart from other crucial elections) had the effect of providing additional time for plotting to mature and for the idea of secession to become domesticated in southern minds.

As for the question of why the mere election of a Republican president should have provided sufficient impulse for disunion, let it be remembered that along with all the southern fears of what might happen after Lincoln took office there was the fear in some quarters that nothing very dramatic would happen at all. Only at this one point in time between the election and inauguration of the first

Republican president was the potential of horror both un-limited *and* untested.   No such clear signal for concerted southern action had ever been sounded before or was ever likely to be sounded again.

DON E. FEHRENBACHER
Professor of History,
Stanford University

The Election of 1896

To many Americans in 1896 the very character and direction of American life would depend upon the outcome of the forthcoming presidential election. To be sure, it long had been customary for the country's political leadership to predict national ruin if the opposing party gained power. The platforms written for earlier campaigns made this clear. In 1876 the Democrats charged the Republicans "with incapacity, waste and fraud," while in 1888 the Republicans accused the Democrats with "criminal nullification of the Constitution" in domestic matters and "inefficiency and cowardice" in foreign affairs. But most citizens had discounted such rhetoric as coming from self-serving politicians who were more interested in their own welfare than in the broader national good.

In 1896, however, the deep sense of unrest and dissatisfaction went far beyond that found in any other presidential election since 1860. Indeed, many people compared the crisis facing the country in 1896 to conditions at the time of Lincoln's election. The factors which threatened national unity were different from those of 1860, but to many Americans they seemed just as real and just as dangerous.

When the national political conventions were held in the summer of 1896, Americans were in their fourth year of depression. Following the financial panic of 1893, hundreds of businesses and industries had gone bankrupt, and others were operating at only partial capacity. Unemployment was widespread and accompanying want and misery had invaded millions of homes. Terrible living conditions, only partly associated with the depression, existed in many cities. Jacob Riis had described the relationship between poverty and poor housing in his book, *How The Other Half Lives,* published in 1890 before the panic began. Agricultural prices were so low that they hardly paid the cost of marketing. Indeed, it was cheaper to burn corn than coal.[1]

The hard times of the 1890's gave rise to demands for federal work relief and governmental action to raise farm prices. Jacob Coxey's march on Washington in 1894, the first people's march on the nation's capitol, was only one manifestation of the increasing calls on government.[2] During the same year, strikes and violence were widespread as workingmen sought to improve their position in the economy. The Pullman strike of July, 1894, thoroughly frightened many Americans. Despite President Cleveland's statement that law and order would be preserved at any cost, when people read the headline about deaths and property destruction, they were overwhelmed with doubts and fears about the country's social stability.[3] It seemed to a growing number of citizens that the nation's social fabric was coming unstuck. Revolutionary radicals were gaining a broader hearing, new political alignments were being made, and the old parties were splintering. The country seemed to be dividing more along economic and class lines than along party lines. To many Americans, this seemed like an ominous situation for the future of the country.

One of the most disturbing things of all was the in-

[1] On the Panic of 1893 and the subsequent depression, see W. J. Lauch, The *Causes of the Panic of 1893* (1907); Samuel Rezneck, "Unemployment, Unrest and Relief in the United States During the Depression of 1893–97," *Jour. Polit. Economy* 61 (August, 1953), and Charles Hoffman "The Depression of the Nineties," *Jour. Econ. History* 16 (June, 1956).

[2] D. L. McMurry, *Coxey's Army* (Boston, Little Brown and Company, 1929).

[3] Almont Lindsey, *The Pullman Strike* (Chicago, University of Chicago Press, 1942); see also New York *Daily Tribune,* July 9 and 10, 1894.

creasing frequency with which basic questions were being asked about the capitalistic system, its operation in the United States, and the distribution of wealth. The Populists had said in 1892 that the system was developing two great classes—tramps and millionaires. The editor of the *Kansas Farmer* wrote in 1894 that the cause of violence and bloodshed was the contest over the possession "of some of God's gifts to men." [4] The Grand Master of the Knights of Labor told a large group of unemployed men in Baltimore in August, 1894, that one class had acquired most of the property while millions starved.[5] In 1895, the master of the Wisconsin State Grange told his depressed listeners that something was radically wrong with "a system under which a few thousand people out of a population of about seventy million have been permitted to absorb more than one-half of the entire wealth of the country and still the process of absorption continues. . . ." [6] These and other critics accused industrial monopoly, the money power, and special interests of perverting the American system. Somehow, they argued, the power of the rich and the super-rich must be curbed.

President Grover Cleveland had no answers to the nation's problems, and he failed completely to attune himself to the growing concerns of an increasing number of citizens. The only response of the Cleveland administration to the depression was repeal of the Sherman Silver Purchase Act and passage of the Wilson-Gorman tariff law which did little more than tinker with tariff rates. While favoring nothing that would command widespread popular support, Cleveland opposed a graduated income tax, mone-

---

4 Quoted in Gilbert C. Fite, "Election of 1896," in Arthur M. Schlesinger, Jr., ed., *The Coming to Power* (New York, Chelsea House, 1972), p. 228. See also Harry P. Robinson, "The Humiliating Report on the Strike Commission," *Forum* 18 (January, 1895): pp. 523–531.

5 Quoted in *Home, Field and Forum* 2 (October, 1894): p. 152.

6 Fite, "Election of 1896," p. 227.

tary inflation, and control of monopoly, objectives desired by so many farmers and workers. With their leadership trying to hold firm against demands for significant change, the Democrats were soundly defeated in the mid-term elections of 1894 when Republicans gained good working majorities in both houses of Congress. Following those elections, more and more Democrats rejected Cleveland's leadership, and throughout 1895 and the early part of 1896, a bitter fight developed for control of the Democratic party.[7]

The man who emerged as the leader among anti-Cleveland Democrats was William Jennings Bryan, the young orator and two-term congressman from Nebraska where the fires of discontent burned hot. Sensing what he believed was great discontent among the common people, Bryan disassociated himself from the old politics of Cleveland and the conservative Democrats, and centered his campaign for the presidential nomination around the money issue. By 1895, the free and unlimited coinage of silver had become the burning question of the day. First pushed by the Populists and other third parties in the West and South, free silver was being advanced as the main antidote to depression and hard times. The free silverites believed that the free and unlimited coinage of silver would increase the money supply, stimulate farm prices, encourage business, and make it easier to pay debts. Throughout 1893 and 1894, a gradual alignment of silver and gold forces occurred which cut across party lines and shattered party unity. In February, 1895, Bryan predicted that "the campaign of

[7] On the growing influence of free silver in the Democratic party, see Allan Nevins, *Grover Cleveland: A Study in Courage* (New York, Dodd, Mead and Co., 1933); J. Rogers Hollingsworth, *The Whirligig of Politics* (Chicago, University of Chicago Press, 1963), and Paul W. Glad, *McKinley, Bryan, and the People* (Philadelphia, J. B. Lippincott Company, 1964). The most complete study of the campaign of 1896 is Stanley Jones, *The Presidential Election of 1896* (Madison, Wis., University of Wisconsin Press, 1964).

1896 will be fought on the money question . . . between the capitalists of the Northeast and the rest of the people of the country." [8]

If this prediction were to be realized, however, the free-silver forces must win control of the national Democratic convention and nominate a man who would lead a campaign on the money issue. While Bryan was among the most active anti-Cleveland leaders, there were many others in the Democratic party who demanded fundamental change and joined in the tussle for party control. Richard (Silver Dick) Bland of Missouri, Senator Joseph Blackburn of Kentucky, Governor Peter Altgeld of Illinois, and a host of others lent their support to state and national efforts to line up delegate support. For example, in Illinois the Cleveland forces sent in some of their big guns, including Secretary of the Treasury John G. Carlisle, to hold the state for the conservatives. After Carlisle spoke in Chicago on the dangers of free silver and the virtues of the gold standard, the editor of the Chicago *Record* said that the secretary had come "fresh from the banquet table of Wall Street goldbugs to tell the idle and starving working men" that robbery was not criminal.[9] Illinois Democrats rode roughshod over the Cleveland men and elected a majority of free silverites to represent them at the forthcoming national convention in Chicago. Hoke Smith, another of Cleveland's cabinet officers, tried to hold Georgia for the president, but a close associate wrote that "all hell couldn't stop" the silver forces in that state.[10]

While the Democrats were dividing over control of their party, the powerful industrial and financial interests in the Republican party were lining up behind William Mc-

[8] Quoted in Paolo E. Coletta, *William Jennings Bryan, Political Evangelist, 1860–1908* (Lincoln, Neb., University of Nebraska Press, 1964), p. 96.

[9] Nevins, *Grover Cleveland*, p. 690.

[10] Dewey W. Grantham, Jr., *Hoke Smith and the Politics of the New South*, (Baton Rouge, Louisiana State University Press, 1958), p. 106.

Kinley. Mark Hanna, the multi-millionaire industrialist from Cleveland, was leaving nothing to chance as he organized the Republican forces behind his fellow Ohioan. It is true that the Republican party was not completely unified, but the western Republicans who favored free silver had no chance whatever of gaining a majority.

McKinley, a former member of the House of Representatives and two-term governor of Ohio, was best known for the tariff law of 1890 and his devotion to the principle of protection of the home market. As he sought his party's nomination, he played down the money question and emphasized the tariff. He argued with considerable skill that times were hard because of the Democratic attack on protection. He declared that a higher tariff would protect farm prices and increase employment by keeping out foreign imports. He was billed as the "advance agent of prosperity." The editor of the *Nation* wrote as early as January, 1895, that it was assuring to hear McKinley talk about economic questions. After listening to the fretting of doomsayers, he wrote, it was pleasant to hear McKinley point the way to prosperity by protecting "our own markets for our manufacturers and agricultural products." [11]

When the Republican convention met in St. Louis on June 16, the Hanna-McKinley machine was in complete control. The McKinleyites had drawn up a platform which, among other things, called for "sound money" which meant the gold standard, and the "uncompromising principle" of tariff protection. The only stir in the smooth-running convention was when Senator Henry Moore Teller of Colorado presented a substitute money plank calling for free silver. The convention promptly rejected the substitute and Senator Teller, with tears in his eyes, marched

[11] The *Nation* 60 (January 31, 1895): p. 81. The best account of McKinley's rise to the Republican nomination is H. Wayne Morgan, *William McKinley and His America* (Syracuse, Syracuse University Press, 1963), chap. 10.

out of the convention with twenty-one silverite delegates behind him. As they left, the other delegates shouted, "Go to Chicago," which was the site of the forthcoming Democratic convention. With this issue removed, the Republicans nominated McKinley on the first ballot.[12]

About a month later, the Democratic delegates descended on the Windy City to approve a platform and nominate a candidate. A few days before the convention opened, Cleveland gold-standard Democrats made a last-ditch effort to derail the free silverites. William C. Whitney, a former secretary of the navy, headed a final effort to commit the party to gold. But he soon saw the futility of such a move. He found the sentiment for silver uncontrollable. As delegates from the South and West stormed from hotel to hotel through the city, Whitney said that "for the first time, I can understand the scenes of the French Revolution."[13]

When the Democratic convention opened on July 7, the free silverites were in decisive control. After seating some contested silver delegates, the convention adopted a platform calling for free and unlimited coinage of silver and gold at a ratio of 16 to 1, a tariff for revenue, and equalized tax burdens.

While Bryan arrived at the convention with substantial support, his famous "Cross of Gold" speech on the platform thrust him into first place. Commenting on the talk, Samuel Gompers, head of the American Federation of Labor, later wrote: "Bryan spoke the language of humanity and he appeared as the proclaimed saviour of the common people. . . ."[14] The delegates nominated him on the fifth ballot.

[12] Elmer Ellis, *Henry Moore Teller, Defender of the West* (Caldwell, Idaho, Caxton Printers, 1941), p. 261.

[13] Nevins, *Grover Cleveland*, p. 700.

[14] Samuel Gompers, *Seventy Years of Life and Labor* (New York, E. P. Dutton and Co., 1925) 2: p. 87.

Other free silverites also quickly rallied to his support. Many pro-silver Republicans announced their backing, and the Populists named Bryan as the official candidate of their party. At the same time, however, gold-standard Democrats forsook their party. They nominated Senator John M. Palmer of Illinois as their official candidate, but most conservative Democrats planned to vote for McKinley.[15]

After a short rest at his home in Lincoln, Nebraska, Bryan began a whirlwind campaign. He went first to New York for a speech in Madison Square Garden. This was what Bryan called enemy country. Realizing that many easterners considered him an irresponsible and dangerous radical, Bryan prepared his address carefully. He assured his audience that neither the Democratic platform nor his own ideas were any threat to private property or social stability. Bryan called for trust in a government of the common people. Then he spent an hour and a half discussing the money question which he said was the "paramount issue" in the campaign.[16] The response to his talk was disappointing, but he continued his stay in New York State for nearly two weeks. As the campaign progressed, Bryan sharpened the issues by talking about power, its distribution and its use in American society. Gold, he said time and again, was the money—or symbol—of entrenched privilege which concentrated economic and political power in the hands of a few; silver was the money—the symbol —demanding a more equal distribution of economic and political power among all of the people. No previous presidential candidate had showed so clearly the direct relationship between economic and political power.[17]

[15] For the best account of the Populists in the campaign, see Robert F. Durden, *The Climax of Populism, The Election of 1896* (Lexington, Kentucky, University of Kentucky Press, 1965), but also see Coletta, *William Jennings Bryan,* pp. 153–160.

[16] New York *Tribune,* August 13, 1896, carried Bryan's speech in full.

[17] Coletta, *William Jennings Bryan,* chap. 9.

From the beginning, Bryan suffered from two major handicaps—lack of money and poor organization. The Democratic National Committee had major offices in Washington, D. C., and Chicago, but both lacked staff and financing. Bryan and other party leaders appealed to the common people for small contributions, but little ever reached party coffers from that source. Western silvermine owners contributed some money, but nothing like the amounts claimed by the Republicans. The usual source of big money for Democratic campaigns was not available because most wealthy members bolted their party.

Despite severe handicaps, Bryan carried on the most extensive campaign in American history up to that time. Appealing to the common people to rescue the nation from the money power and special interests, he traveled some 18,000 miles and delivered hundreds of speeches. Crowds of 25,000 and 50,000 were not uncommon. Emotionalism often ran high as Bryan took on the role of a national savior. "No matter what may be the result," a Texas friend wrote, "you will be greater than any other man since Christ." [18]

While Bryan traveled extensively calling for fundamental redistribution of wealth and power, McKinley conducted a calm, unruffled campaign from his front porch in Canton, Ohio. He relied heavily on the organization put together by Mark Hanna and financed lavishly by big business. From their headquarters in New York and Chicago, the Republicans established organizations down to the local level. They sent out hundreds of speakers and distributed tons of literature attacking free silver, a low tariff, and Bryan's irresponsibility.[19]

There was no lack of funds to finance even the most

18 *Ibid.,* p. 188.
19 Morgan, *William McKinley,* pp. 223–243.

elaborate effort. Standard Oil Company gave $250,000, each of the four big meat packers contributed $100,000, and other representatives of American industrial power gave hundreds of thousands more. Charles G. Dawes, the young Chicago financier who handled party finances, recorded in his diary on September 11 that Hanna had handed him $50,000 in cash, the contribution of an unnamed railway company.[20]

While the nationwide organization operated smoothly and effectively, McKinley met with scores of visiting delegations at his home. Farmers, workers, businessmen and other groups were brought to Canton to hear McKinley expound on issues of concern to them. While consistently denouncing free silver, McKinley put more and more stress on the tariff as the campaign advanced. He contrasted the country's prosperity before Cleveland took office in 1893 with the economic hardship that followed the inauguration of a Democratic administration. The cause of the difficulty, McKinley said, was the Democratic tariff. McKinley skillfully wove together the protective tariff, prosperity, and the Republican party. He argued that protection would restore industrial prosperity which in turn would increase employment. That would expand the demand for farm products, thereby raising prices and helping farmers. McKinley was a master at presenting the home market argument made popular years before by Henry Clay. He accused the Democrats of free trade, which favored foreigners, and he associated protectionism with patriotism and nationalism. Throughout the campaign, McKinley explained that the principles advocated by Bryan were a threat to America's basic institutions. He denounced the idea of economic classes and called for national unity. To talk of classes and conflict of interests between rich and poor, be-

---

[20] Charles G. Dawes, *A Journal of the McKinley Years* (Chicago, Lakeside Press, 1950), p. 97.

tween capital and labor, between farmers and bankers was, he said, most reprehensible.[21]

The outcome on November 3 was a comfortable victory for McKinley who received 51 per cent of the vote compared to 46 per cent for Bryan. The remainder of the votes went to the candidates of minor parties. McKinley's strength was concentrated in New England, the Middle Atlantic States, and the Old Northwest. He ran ahead of Bryan in the principal industrial states and in the older, more prosperous commercial farming areas between Pennsylvania and Iowa. These were the centers of economic power which the Republicans had translated into political power during this crucial election.

What factors accounted for the McKinley victory? In the first place, the Republicans had a momentum which they carried on from the midterm elections of 1894 when they swept both houses of Congress. This political trend was intensified by efficient organization and the expenditure during the campaign of six to ten times as much money as the Democrats. Moreover, Bryan had to carry the heavy weight of a divided party and hard times. "I have borne the sins of Grover Cleveland," [22] Bryan wrote. Furthermore, the Republican party was the majority party in 1896, and to win Bryan had to attract Republican votes. Not only did he fail to do this in key states, he did not even have the support of conservative Democrats who could have given him money and organizational talent. Bryan's emphasis on free silver did not appeal to workingmen who feared that inflationary farm prices would bring about rising food costs. Labor was more impressed with McKinley's promise to revive industry and create jobs by raising the tariff. Likewise, many farmers, especially in

21 New York *Tribune*, August 27, 1896.
22 Quoted by Coletta, *William Jennings Bryan*, p. 197.

the Old Northwest, were impressed with McKinley's home-market argument.

Perhaps as much as anything the outcome of the election was decided by the image of the candidates. Despite his conservative nature and devout Christian character, Bryan was portrayed by his opponents as a wild-eyed radical who was unsafe to govern the country. Republicans labeled him an anarchist, socialist, and demagogue. His backers were compared to the Revolutionary hordes in France in the early 1790's. On the other hand, Republicans were successful in presenting McKinley as the defender of basic American institutions and traditions. To support McKinley was to back the principles of law and order, the protection of property, and social stability. McKinley regularly referred to the dangerous and revolutionary assaults on law and order, and associated seeming social disintegration with Bryan and the Democrats. "Government by law must first be assured," he said in his acceptance speech. "Everything else can wait. The spirit of lawlessness must be extinguished by the fires of an unselfish and lofty patriotism." The Democrats, he continued, were attacking the "public faith." [23] Throughout the campaign, Republicans acted as though they and they alone could save American civilization from the onslaught of radicals and anarchists. Bishop Ireland of St. Paul said on October 12 that to support McKinley was to work for "the integrity of the nation, for social order, . . . for the honor of America and the permanency of free institutions." [24] Thus McKinley and the gold standard became the symbols of Americanism, nationalism, patriotism, and social stability. No amount of oratory by Bryan could overcome the manufactured image that he was a dangerous rabble-rouser who was a threat to American institutions.

[23] New York *Tribune*, August 27, 1896.
[24] Quoted in Kokomo (Indiana) *Daily Tribune*, October 12, 1896.

Bryan failed to develop trust and confidence in himself or his party, while McKinley appeared to be a solid, stable, and trustworthy leader in whose hands America would be safe. That is the basic and fundamental reason why the people elected William McKinley president in 1896.[25]

GILBERT C. FITE
President, Eastern Illinois University

[25] Between 1894 and the presidential election two years later, editorial and magazine writers dealt extensively with the law and order issue. For insights into the issue of social and political stability, see the *New York Tribune,* June 22, July 24, August 25, September 9, September 25 and November 6, 1896; The Galveston *Daily News,* June 17 and July 10; W. E. Chandler, "Issues and Prospects of the Campaign," *North American Review* 163 (August, 1896): pp. 175–182; "The Political Menace of Discontent," *Atlantic Monthly* (October, 1896), pp. 447–451; and the *Commercial and Financial Chronicle,* 63 (July 11, 1896): p. 48.

The Election of 1936

T HE WORD "CRUCIAL" is defined by *Webster's New Collegiate Dictionary* as being the "final determination of a doubtful issue," and thus is easily applied to a number of American elections. Of course, in a sense, all elections are crucial, in that they determine some question, whether it be who is to hold office, the composition of a party, or the success and nature of an issue. It is also clear that elections in some years are more important than those in others, just as a presidential election is more important than a contest for alderman.

Historians generally agree that the national elections of 1800, 1836, 1860, 1896, and 1936 are among the most crucial. That of 1800 was crucial in that it demonstrated that an election could lead to the peaceful transfer of governmental authority from one party to another. Moreover, the election indicated the durability of the Democratic Republicans, who would, in one form or another, be the dominant political party in the United States until 1860 and the champions of a relatively weak federal authority which would permit governance to be largely carried on by state and local governments. The election of 1836 was less important, but still crucial, for it made plain that national elections would be decided by popular vote and that the chief opposition would be the Whig party. In effect, 1836 manifested the existence of the popular two-party system of national politics and government which has characterized the United States since then. The election of 1860 is a landmark of the proportions of 1800. In 1860 it was shown that neither the dominant party—the Democrats—nor the nation could stand as it had been,

divided against itself. Furthermore, the electoral success
of the Republicans in 1860 gave them the chance for political dominance during the following generation and
therefore the opportunity, though not often seized, to act
upon their bespoken policy of heightened activity by the
federal government. The 1896 election, like that of 1836,
was on a lower level of significance, but it did feature a
national party, the Democrats, that called for a more active
national government. That election also marked a considerable realignment of elements within the two major
parties; the effective death of a movement, the Populists,
that might have replaced one of the two major parties or
might even have started the United States on the path to
a three-party system; and the beginning of a sixteen-year
period of strong control of the federal government by the
Republicans.

The election of 1912 should be considered for status as
a crucial election, albeit a lesser one. Some realignment
of forces was started then, but, more important, 1912 in-
augurated a twenty-year period in which American politics
swung wildly from leadership by one major party to another and back again in 1920 and then, in 1932, once more
in the other direction. Considerable fluctuation also took
place regarding ideas as to what the government's role
should be, and the period was marked by a not unrelated
high level of third-party activity. In other words, the 1912
election was not so much crucial in terms of what it led to
as it was in marking the beginning of two decades in which
no party or set of new political ideas was dominant.

In brief, politics in the United States has been marked
by certain elections that were critical in the evolution of
how transfers of power would occur, who would benefit or
lose significantly from them, or what the role of government would be. Each of these elections was a point at
which a change took place that had major ramifications

for the American people as well as a point at which an earlier stage in the evolution of national politics and government was shown to have been considered wanting. They demonstrated the flexibility of the form of politics sketched in state and national constitutions, and the success of the founding fathers in establishing a system that would —with the exception of the Civil War—avoid the use of violence to decide among the policies and the leaders at issue. In other words, revolution in the United States had become institutionalized, breaking out regularly every four years, using ballots instead of bullets.

In looking at the election of 1936, one must first dispose of the question of why 1936 instead of 1932 was crucial. The election of 1932 was remarkable in that it represented a great swing of popular support from the Republicans to the Democrats, but that signified only a rejection of the incumbents, since it was unclear what the victorious Democrats stood for beyond gaining office and doing something about the Great Depression. Moreover, there had not been a definite realignment of political elements within the United States. Given this, 1932 resembles the congressional elections of 1894 or the national election of 1856. As in those contests, change had occurred in 1932, but nothing had yet been settled that would affect the United States over a long period of time. The national election of 1936 would be the crucial juncture.

The politics of 1936 seemed crucial even to those involved in it. The parties were in flux, in terms of both their composition and their policies. Nationally prominent Republicans would support the Democratic ticket, nationally prominent Democrats would endorse the Republican nominees, and third-party movements were abundant. Where all this would lead, no one knew. Everyone, however, seemed to predict dire results unless his favorite candidate won at the polls. Many of Franklin D. Roosevelt's supporters asserted that the election of a Republican would lead to fascism or at least the return of the worst of the depression.   Many Republicans declared that, if Roosevelt were reelected, the consequence would be the end of constitutional government.   Felix Frankfurter wrote to Harold Ickes that the fate of the Western world was at stake: "the president's reelection will hearten and invigorate the forces of democracy, while Landon's victory will encourage all the anti-democratic forces."   Robert R. McCormick's anti-New Deal *Chicago Tribune* daily reminded its readers of the number of days left before the election in which "to save your country." [1]   Although these apprehensions were overstated, they mirrored a concern for America's future reminiscent of the deeply troubled feelings of the 1850's.   They reflected the widespread conviction that the election would decide what the United States, and perhaps the world, would be like for years to come.

The course and results of election campaigns are substantially affected by events taking place well before the nomination of candidates.   The 1936 election was no exception.   By early indications, it was by no means sure who would win or even who would participate in the election. There was the threat that Senator Huey Long, the Louisiana demagogue, would run for president, and a Democratic National Committee poll indicated that he would be a strong contender.   Assassination removed him, however, as a political force in August, 1935.   There was also the possibility that elements left of the New Deal might coalesce into a national farmer-labor party.   And this was not an insignificant possibility, for Farmer-Laborites controlled the government of Minnesota, Progressives dominated that of Wisconsin, radical candidates had polled a majority of

[1] Donald R. McCoy, *Landon of Kansas* (Lincoln, Neb., 1966), pp. 262–264, 347; Felix Frankfurter to Harold L. Ickes, October 28, 1936, Papers of Harold L. Ickes, Manuscript Division, Library of Congress.

votes for governor in California in 1934, and many national labor unions had adopted resolutions calling for a new national party. Moreover, the non-Communist groups, despite their differences in priorities, were in touch with one another, and they were far from pleased with the works of the Democratic party. There were signs that former Democratic presidential nominees Alfred Smith and John W. Davis and Governors Albert Ritchie of Maryland and Eugene Talmadge of Georgia were thinking of forming a conservative "Jeffersonian Democratic" party in opposition to Roosevelt. Big business also was plainly unhappy with the New Deal. In January, 1936, the Gallup poll recorded only 50 per cent of its respondents in favor of the New Deal and only 51 per cent inclining toward electing Democrats to the Senate.[2]

The president was concerned and acted to meet political dissatisfaction. In September, 1935, he declared that there would be a "breathing spell" for business, for the New Deal program to cope with depression "has now reached substantial completion." For the left, Roosevelt apparently hoped that the results of his program would either placate or deflate them. It was plain by early 1936, however, that he was not enlisting the support of either the right or the left. He needed a new strategy. What he devised was the idea of sponsoring little new government action, but of discussing whatever was done militantly. Thus might he court both the right and the left. That strategem was seen in his January message to Congress, in which he deplored the grasping for power of the "resplen-

[2] James A. Farley, *Behind the Ballots: The Personal History of a Politician* (New York, 1938), pp. 249–250; Farley, *Jim Farley's Story: The Roosevelt Years* (New York, 1948), pp. 50–51; Donald R. McCoy, *Angry Voices: Left-of-Center Politics in the New Deal Era* (Lawrence, Kansas, 1958), chaps. III-IV; Hadley Cantril and Mildred Strunk (eds.), *Public Opinion, 1935–1946* (Princeton, 1951), pp. 978, 932.

dent economic autocracy," and yet called for a balanced budget that would require no new taxes.

The Supreme Court and Congress combined, however, to mangle Roosevelt's political plans. The invalidation of the Agricultural Adjustment Act in January required not only that the government return $200 million in taxes to farm product processors, but that the administration formulate a new farm program, which in itself was bound to stir up antagonisms. Congress passed, over the president's veto, authorization to make bonus payments of almost two billion dollars to veterans. This meant that Roosevelt had little choice but to ask for higher taxes. He responded by requesting a tax on undistributed corporate profits. Congress was unhappy with this, but finally enacted a compromise, in the Revenue Act of 1936, which increased regular corporation taxes and put a nominal tax on undistributed corporate profits. Although this intensified the enmity of big business toward the administration, it had the advantages of avoiding raising taxes on the mass of citizens and creating the illusion for many on the left that the president was genuinely hostile to big business. The legislation also contributed to heightened economic activity, by forcing big business to spend some of its reserves in order to avoid paying the undistributed profits tax, as did the infusion into the economy of the bonus payment.[3] The improving economy kept the center in the president's camp and siphoned off popular support from the left for Roosevelt.

By May, the left was in dire straits. Much of the Socialist party's depression-inflated following had gone over to the New Deal, and part of what remained was in

[3] James MacGregor Burns, *Roosevelt: The Lion and the Fox* (New York, 1956), pp. 226, 334; Arthur M. Schlesinger, Jr., *The Politics of Upheaval, 1935–1936* (Boston, 1960), pp. 504–509; William E. Leuchtenburg, *Franklin D. Roosevelt and the New Deal, 1932–1940* (New York, 1963), pp. 170–172.

the process of transferring to a new third party, the American Labor party, as a way to remain independent and yet vote for Roosevelt. A convention, assembled in May to discuss the formation of a coalition national third party, found that the Socialists and Townsendites refused to cooperate; that the Wisconsin Progressive and Minnesota Farmer-Labor parties had decided not to support anything that might jeopardize Roosevelt's election, for fear of what the alternative might be; and that the Farm Holiday Association's interest in third-party action had dwindled since the death of its dynamic leader, Milo Reno. As with socialism, what remained of native radicalism was divided in its goals. Moreover, the Communists, whose ranks were also being depleted, were trying to run their own united front movement, which further hurt the appeal of a native radical coalition. This all reflected that (1) radical followings had fallen off substantially during the first part of 1936 as the New Deal's achievements looked more attractive, and (2) most of those who were left in the radical folds of the body politic were unwilling to support a third-party presidential candidacy that might draw enough votes from Roosevelt to lead to the election of, as Minnesota's Farmer-Labor Governor Floyd Olson put it, "a fascist Republican." [4]

Yet the Roosevelt forces were far from feeling safe. The varying results of public-opinion polls gave the Democrats no comfort. Furthermore, the Roosevelt administration was the whipping boy for many elements, including some independents, many conservative Democrats, most Republican leaders, most businessmen, and most newspaper editorialists. Indeed, since newspapers were still often regarded as having great influence in affecting voters' decisions, there was some Democratic concern for their gen-

[4] David A. Shannon, *The Socialist Party of America: A History* (New York, 1955), pp. 242–247; McCoy, *Angry Voices*, pp. 105–112.

erally anti-New Deal position.   (One of the important results of the 1936 election was to smash this myth once and for all.)[5]

In early June the Republicans met in Cleveland to formulate their platform and to choose their nominees for president and vice-president.   As it turned out, the party was to constitute the chief opposition and the only real alternative to Roosevelt.   It was, however, a bundle of contradictions and complexes.   The Republicans included leaders who ranged all the way from the big-business *laissez-faire* views of former Pennsylvania Senator Joseph Grundy to the ultra-liberal position of Senator William E. Borah of Idaho.   It was a party that, on the one hand, feared it could not win because of the severe defeats dealt it in 1932 and 1934, but yet, on the other hand, thought that it might have a chance because various indicators showed that Roosevelt was only marginally popular.   Regular Republican leaders were sure that the improving economy would unleash voters from a feeling of dependence upon the New Deal, and yet they were equally certain that the economic upswing would make the New Deal unassailably popular by election day.   In short, Republican self-confidence varied wildly from faction to faction, from man to man, and even from day to day.

The platform and the nominees, in effect, were compromises, reflecting the wide range of opinion within the party and yet also mirroring the recognition of most Republican leaders that the party could not return to 1932.

[5] George Wolfskill and John A. Hudson, *All but the People: Franklin D. Roosevelt and His Critics, 1933–1939* (New York, 1969), chap. VII; Schlesinger, *The Politics of Upheaval*, p. 633; William E. Leuchtenburg, "Election of 1936," in Arthur M. Schlesinger, Jr., and Fred L. Israel (eds.), *History of American Presidential Elections, 1789–1968* (4 v., New York, 1971) 3: p. 2847. The best-known polls were not in agreement. For example, in October the *Literary Digest* survey gave Landon 54.8 per cent and Roosevelt 40.7 per cent and the Gallup poll gave them, respectively, 44.2 and 50.3 per cent. *Topeka Daily Capital,* October 23, 1936; Cantril and Strunk, *Public Opinion,* p. 591.

Although the platform fiercely condemned the New Deal, it conceded the need for federal support of relief programs, called for old-age pensions, and endorsed state unemployment insurance. Labor's rights to organize and to bargain collectively were recognized, farmers were promised a large parcel of benefits, and regulation of unsavory business practices was pledged. After a mild fight for the presidential nomination, the Republicans chose Alfred M. Landon, the able, moderate two-term governor of Kansas to be their standard-bearer. Another former Theodore Roosevelt Progressive, Frank Knox, the publisher of the *Chicago News,* was nominated for vice-president.[6]

The Democratic national convention met in Philadelphia in late June. The meeting offered no surprises. It was clear that the ticket again would be Franklin D. Roosevelt and John Nance Garner. It was also plain that the platform would be drafted in the White House, subject to only minor alterations in the convention. The Democratic platform damned the Republicans, extravagantly praised the New Deal, and pledged to continue and even extend the policies adopted during Roosevelt's first term.

The main issues of the 1936 campaign were fairly well drawn in the conventions and in the acceptance speeches of the major-party presidential nominees. The stated goals of Roosevelt and the Democratic party were to complete the tasks of bringing about the recovery of economic prosperity, of reforming the government and the economy so that all would have prosperity and that none would have a privileged status, and of providing relief to those in need until recovery had been attained. There were also the promises of items dear to business, a balanced budget and debt reduction. Yet the Democrats left no doubt who was responsible for the country's economic problems. As

[6] McCoy, *Landon of Kansas,* pp. 253–261, *passim.*

Roosevelt indicated in his acceptance speech at Philadelphia's Franklin Field, it was the "economic royalists," who were seeking a "new industrial dictatorship" in America.[7] Governor Landon and the Republican party declared that a calming hand was necessary to give business, under regulatory guidelines, the opportunity to revive so that it could generate prosperity throughout the land, so that Americans could reach the "new frontier" which science and technology promised. While this was underway, a Republican administration would provide relief to the country's needy. Agriculture would be given incentives to reach stability, through the development of new markets, conservation, and the encouragement of the family farm and more widespread farm ownership.[8]

It was also in June that a new, unorthodox element injected itself into the campaign. When the native radicals decided not to run a national campaign, the way seemed open for another movement to challenge the major parties. That was a coalition of the forces led by Father Charles Coughlin, the popular radio priest, Dr. Francis Townsend, the champion of pensions for the aged, and the fundamentalist preacher Gerald L. K. Smith, the former organizer of Huey Long's Share-Our-Wealth group. The resultant Union party named a veteran agrarian congressman, William Lemke of North Dakota, for president. The new party's leaders claimed that they would attract between five and fifteen million votes. Although that was an exaggeration, there was the possibility that the Union party could pull enough votes from Roosevelt to throw the election to Landon.

Some Democrats were understandably alarmed and ac-

---

[7] Leuchtenburg, "Election of 1936," pp. 2828–2829; Schlesinger, *The Politics of Upheaval*, pp. 579–585.

[8] *Official Report of the Proceedings of the Twenty-first Republican National Convention* (New York, 1936), *passim;* McCoy, *Landon of Kansas*, pp. 272–273, 283.

cordingly took action to counteract the possible appeal of
the Union party among Catholics, fundamentalist Prot-
estants, the aged, farmers, and the poor. There was also
a movement within the Catholic Church to combat the
threat of Coughlinism to the president's reelection campaign. Democratic and Catholic efforts were strongly
augmented by those of Socialists, Communists, and most
non-Marxist radicals, who saw in the new party a threat
to their political strength as well as a disruptive force that
might cause Landon's election. There need not have
been much worry, for what Norman Thomas labeled "a
union of two and a half Messiahs plus some neo-Populists"
contained the seeds of its own abysmal failure. The dem-
agogic, bigoted, and often contradictory statements of the
Union party's leaders, as well as their incompatible back-
grounds, were too much for even their own admirers to
swallow.[9] What is really important about the Union party
was that it helped to invigorate its various opponents into
action to head off the threats to Roosevelt's reelection that
it seemed to present.

The 1936 Democratic and Republican campaigns were
of different pieces. The shift of city voters to the Democrats, first observed in 1928, had greatly accelerated during
the 1930's, partly as urban blacks abandoned the Republicans between 1932 and 1936. The Republicans had also
lost much of their labor, farmer, and even small-business
backing, and they had lost federal patronage and had few
state and local governmental resources to command. Only
the so-called Jeffersonian Democrats, ladened more with
elder statesmen than with corps of voters, were coming to
their support. Therefore, Governor Landon and his aides

---

[9] David H. Bennett, *Demagogues in the Depression: American Radicals
and the Union Party, 1932–1936* (New Brunswick, N. J., 1969), *passim;* McCoy,
Angry Voices, pp. 141–152; George Q. Flynn, *American Catholics & the Roosevelt Presidency, 1932–1936* (Lexington, Ky., 1968), pp. 209–230.

planned a vigorous campaign to try to recapture what the Republican party had lost since 1930.

Thanks to fervent big-business and newspaper support, the Republicans were not without resources to contest the election. This plus the dedication of Landon and National Committee Chairman John D. M. Hamilton allowed new life to be pumped into the shriveled organs of Republicanism. Almost daily the Republican leaders held press conferences, and they often took to the radio. Landon and Knox made national speaking tours, and their headquarters flooded the nation with political advertising. Landon's campaign emphasized his positive and progressive points of view. The Kansas governor forthrightly denounced religious bigotry and racial prejudice. He contradicted publisher William Randolph Hearst, one of his leading supporters, by rejecting the use of loyalty oaths for teachers. He enthusiastically endorsed conservation, drought relief, and aid to tenant farmers. Landon stressed that unemployment relief and old-age pensions would be given to those who needed them. He promised to balance the federal budget, although not by depriving any American of needed assistance. It would be accomplished by "cutting out waste and extravagance" and eliminating the use of public funds for political purposes. Furthermore, Landon declared that a well-administered, soundly financed government could promote legitimate and rapid business expansion, thereby providing the economic growth necessary to attain full employment.

Landon's generally reasonable campaign was, however, impaired by the shrill charges of Knox, Herbert Hoover, and the Jeffersonian Democrats that the Roosevelt administration was dismantling the Constitution, eroding the people's character, and leading the nation in the direction of dictatorship. These cries were seldom accompanied by constructive discussion of how the Republicans would help the country recover from depression or avoid the New Deal's excesses. Even Landon, toward the end of the campaign, indulged increasingly in negative criticism of the administration.[10] The overall impression was that the Republicans had two contradictory goals, running the New Deal right and wholly repealing the New Deal.

The Democratic effort relied more on organization than on the campaigning of Roosevelt and Garner. Although the New Deal had only about nine million dollars in campaign funds compared with fourteen million for the Republicans,[11] its funds were effectively used to publicize the Democratic administration, its promises, and particularly its many accomplishments. Additionally significant was the vastly superior patronage manpower available to Roosevelt and his campaign managers. Because the Democrats were in power in Washington and in most places over the country, their ranks included an unusually large number of elected and appointed officials. Eager to keep their jobs, these officeholders feverishly went about telling voters the good news of the New Deal.

An outstanding feature of the Democratic campaign was the use of auxiliary groups to rally voters. Organized labor was encouraged to establish Labor's Non-Partisan League. The Progressive National Committee was formed to appeal to liberal Republicans and independents on Roosevelt's behalf, and the Good Neighbor League attracted educators, Negroes, women, religious leaders, and civic-minded businessmen. These and five lesser auxiliary committees enlisted the talents and energies of thousands of reputable Americans in the president's cause, people who otherwise would have had little or nothing to do with the Democratic party. Their presence in the campaign

10 McCoy, *Landon of Kansas*, chaps. 11–13.
11 *Senate Investigation of Campaign Expenditures in 1936*, Report 151, 75th Cong., 1st sess. (Washington, 1937), pp. 27, 29.

allowed Roosevelt's campaign managers to reach voters who were seldom caught up in electioneering. The auxiliary groups also offered a halfway house to encourage and shelter those who were shifting from other parties or from independent status to the Democrats. It should be noted that the auxiliary groups helped significantly to remove political independence from the national scene for over a decade and along with it progressivism as it had evolved during the 1920's and early 1930's.[12]

Yet the Democrats were not just relying on the auxiliaries to tap new sources of votes. The Democratic National Committee through its own units encouraged the realignment of voters. Particularly outstanding in this respect was the work of the Committee's Women's Division, headed by Mary Dewson, to recruit women for service in Roosevelt's army of political salvation. The administration's efforts to work Catholics, Jews, and blacks into government and party positions were also of great significance. As National Committee Chairman James A. Farley said, "We began at the first of the year and never let up until the polls closed ten months later. We tried not to miss a single trick. We didn't miss many." [13]

Of course, Roosevelt himself was the keystone of the Democratic campaign. He was a leader who could make most Americans feel that he knew their problems, hopes, and aspirations, and, equally important, that he intended to do something about them. He was no Jeremiah, for he believed that problems could be solved. He recognized that he could sometimes be guilty of sins of omission (sins of commission were exclusively reserved for his opponents),

[12] Donald R. McCoy, "The Progressive National Committee of 1936," *Western Political Quart.* 9 (1956): pp. 454–469; McCoy, "The Good Neighbor League and the Presidential Election of 1936," *Western Political Quart.* 13 (1960): pp. 1011–1021.

[13] Leuchtenburg, "Election of 1936," pp. 2830–2835; Flynn, *American Catholics & the Roosevelt Presidency*, pp. 50–55; Farley, *Jim Farley's Story*, p. 58.

but he appeared willing to make up for them. His sense of humor made him seem warmly human. He had also found a scapegoat for the depression in big business and the Republicans, and it was a believable scapegoat the way he pictured it.

Until late September, Roosevelt contented himself with "nonpolitical" tours and overseeing political strategy-making. Even then his overt campaigning before the election was not intensive, for he gave only a handful of speeches. In them he reiterated his administration's record and renewed his pledge to serve as the champion of the people and the enemy of the "forces of selfishness." The president also occasionally twitted Governor Landon for promising to cut federal spending and yet to operate a large program of government services. As Roosevelt said, "You cannot be an old-guard Republican in the east, and a New Deal Republican in the west. You cannot promise to repeal taxes before one audience and promise to spend more of the taxpayers' money before another audience." [14]

All in all, the 1936 campaign was exciting and intense. Charges, highly seasoned with invective, were hurled at one's opponents on any and almost all occasions. Almost every politician stood ready to tell the public and the press of the enemy's faults in spectacular detail. A majority of Americans accepted the proposition that the Republicans and business were solely and possibly criminally responsible for the depression; a substantial minority seemed willing to believe that the Democrats were ruining the nation in a way that would lead, unwittingly or intentionally, to totalitarianism. Personalities were readily besmirched. Roosevelt was "that man," the evil genius in the White House; Landon had sold out to Wall Street.

[14] Schlesinger, *The Politics of Upheaval*, chaps. 32–34; Burns, *Roosevelt*, chap. 14; McCoy, *Landon of Kansas*, p. 308.

Both were allegedly surrounded by agents of deceit, who if anything were more evil than their principals.

In effect, civil war raged in the United States in 1936, but it was fought within the confines of the electoral system, and with words and paper instead of gunpowder and steel. It was not a case, as it had been in some earlier elections, of one section of the country against other sections, or of country folk against city-dwellers, or even of the young against the old. It was the closest that America had come to class warfare, as labor was arrayed almost solidly against business, as the poor were pitted against the well-fixed, and as the middle class was split against itself. This was the consequence of the ravages of depression, which made Americans sharply aware of their economic position. It was augmented by the inability of most politicians at the time to resist indulging in demagoguery. Several earlier election campaigns had been as unrestrained in the use of invective and distortion, but the impact was vastly greater in 1936 because of the amplification of remarks by radio, sound film, and loudspeakers.[15]

Roosevelt and the Democrats won a smashing victory. The president polled 27,752,869 votes to 16,674,665 for Landon. Indeed, the margin in the Electoral College was even more stunning, as the Kansas governor carried only the eight votes of Maine and Vermont. The Democrats further extended their great majority in Congress, as the number of Republican senators plummeted from 25 to 16 and of representatives from 103 to 89. Still worse was the devastation wrought on third parties. William Lemke and the Union party attracted only 882,479 votes and Socialist Norman Thomas and Communist Earl Browder, respectively, polled only 187,720 and 80,159.[16]

[15] Schlesinger, *The Politics of Upheaval*, chaps. 32–34; Burns, *Roosevelt*, chap. 14; McCoy, *Landon of Kansas*, chaps. 11–12.

[16] Bureau of the Census, U.S. Department of Commerce, *Historical Statistics of the United States: Colonial Times to 1957* (Washington, 1960), pp. 682, 691.

The very fact that there was long some question about Roosevelt's reelection was one great contributing factor to the Democratic landslide. Democrats and Roosevelt supporters among independents, Republicans, and third-party people were early agitated by the possibility of the president's defeat and they went forth in remarkably energetic ways to ensure his reelection. Organization, patronage, and publicity were highly effectively used, and previously lightly involved or uninvolved citizens were appealed to as never before. The public was approached with the fervor of an evangelical movement. More important, the public was receptive to the approaches and energy expended in trying to enlist their support. Despite vigorous efforts by the Republicans and the Union party, the Democratic ticket proved invincible.

Landon never had a chance. His side just did not have the resources, issues, or prestige to overcome the Roosevelt record and campaign. Under the circumstances, Landon probably did as good a job as could have been expected. He received almost a million more popular votes than Hoover had in 1932 and carried 87 more counties.[17] Moreover, he and his associates reinvigorated the Republican party organization and gave it positive as well as carping issues to merchandise.

The consequences of the 1936 election were plain the day after the polls closed. The Democratic party had been genuinely reconstituted. No longer was it a sectional party with outposts here and there in the North and West. It was fully national, and it was that way because Roosevelt had put together and solidified a remarkable coalition of voters, including labor, blacks, ethnic groups, religious minorities, the poor, large numbers of farmers, and many men in small business. The New Deal coalition also swept up legions of women, youth, intellectuals, and

---

[17] McCoy, *Landon of Kansas*, p. 340.

city folk who did not belong in the above categories, along with many professionals and large blocs of civil servants. True, much of this had come together in 1932. It was clear by 1936, however, that the shift was even larger than in 1932 and, more important, that it was not just "a sometime thing." The new coalition was to last for at least a generation. It made the Democratic party the dominant party, a role it had not occupied since before the Civil War.

More significant, the election of 1936 confirmed that big government was here to stay, that Americans were now looking more often to Washington for the solution of their problems instead of to themselves, the city hall, or the state capitol. That this was true was indicated by the shift of the Republicans, in their platform and in Governor Landon's statements, to support of a greatly increased role for the federal government. Along with this as a matter of course came the era of big federal spending and high taxes. Landon might have talked about balancing the budget, as Roosevelt occasionally did, but neither of them was speaking about reducing the revenue yield.

One other major result was that Americans, by re-maining committed to the Democratic and Republican parties, perpetuated at a time of economic crisis and po-litical unsettledness not only the two-party system but also the concept of deciding national differences at the polls. Moreover, they showed themselves eager to accept scattered remedies and reforms rather than risk a thorough-going change of the system. This was, in the long run, the most fateful decision that the people made, for at no time in the nation's history were circumstances so ripe for in-stituting revolutionary economic and political changes. In effect, Americans showed their faith in abiding by con-stitutional politics and government and their willingness to amend rather than scrap the capitalistic mass-production-consumption economy.

In these, and in other ways, such as the further infusion of class conflict in the political dialogue, the election of 1936 did determine much of what the United States would be like for decades to come, and with considerable impact on the world as well. Because of that, it was clearly a crucial election.

DONALD R. McCOY
Professor of History,
University of Kansas

INDEX